M000074674

HOW TO DO AN
INTERVENTION

A STEP-BY-STEP
GUIDE FOR PARENTS

By Marc Kantor,
Certified Intervention Professional (CIP)

Copyright © 2020 All rights reserved. No part of this publication can be reproduced or transmitted in any form or by any means, electronic or mechanical, without permission in writing from the author or publisher.

ISBN-13: 978-1-951407-31-5
ISBN-13: 978-1-951407-30-8 (ebook)

In memory of Bob Elias, I am forever grateful to you for finding me and speaking in a language I could understand.

With gratitude and love to the people who kept loving me long after I stopped loving myself—my wife Julie, my daughter Justine, my parents Mel and Carole, my sister Zena and everybody else who has walked alongside me.

Contents

Introduction	xi
Understanding Addiction	xvii
Codependency and Enabling	xxv
1. PREPARATIONS FOR INTERVENTION	1
Getting Started	1
Take Care with Timing	5
Every Intervention is Unique	7
Don't Blame Yourself	9
Doing Your Own Intervention Is a Risk	9
First Steps	11
Scheduling and Logistics	13
Inviting and Screening Participants	18
How Many People Should Come to an Intervention?	20
Confirming Insurance Benefits (In-Network vs. Out-of-Network) and Paying for Treatment	25
Selecting a Treatment Center	30
Length of Treatment	35
Mental Illness and Dual Diagnosis	38
Geography Matters	38
Pre-Intervention and Intervention Agendas	40
Arranging Transportation to Treatment	42
Writing an Impact Letter	46

Use a Timeline to Demonstrate The   51
Problem
Choosing and Implementing   53
Consequences
Selecting Venues   56
Getting Help for Yourself and Other   57
Family Members

2. THE INTERVENTION   59
Who Should Lead the Intervention?   59
Meeting Before the Intervention   60
When Your Child Enters the Room   63
Drug Testing and Narcan   64
What if They Run?   65
Reading Impact Letters   66
After Reading Impact Letters   67
If They Hesitate or Refuse to Go   68
The Turning Point   73
Common Excuses for Refusing   75
Treatment

3. POST-INTERVENTION AND   84
ADDITIONAL RESOURCES
Intervention Follow-Up   84
When Treatment Ends   89
Sober Living   91
The First Year of Recovery   92

Conclusion   94
Additional Resources   97
Exhibit 1: Sobriety Agreement   99
Exhibit 2: Meditations   104
About the Author   107

"I think love is the most durable element in the world, and my whole approach is based on that."
   -Rev. Martin Luther King, Jr.

Introduction

Congratulations on taking the first step towards getting your son or daughter the help they need to overcome their addiction to drugs and alcohol. Like most parents seeking solutions for their children's addiction and associated mental health problems, you have likely not arrived here easily. It's been my experience that parents of addicted children, regardless of their children's age, are often subjected to long periods of erratic behavior, sleepless nights, anxiety, hopelessness, calls from the police and even stressful trips to the hospital or psych ward.

By the time a parent contacts me they are often traumatized, exhausted and dumbfounded. Not only have they been put through the ringer, they've even been abused by their own child. It's not uncommon for me to hear stories of parents being victimized by their addicted children, including verbal abuse and sometimes physical abuse.

Throughout this book, I frequently refer to drugs and alcohol but I am generally speaking about any addiction, regardless of substance. If your child is addicted to pain pills or suffers from Binge Eating Disorder (BED), please do not dismiss it because it doesn't exactly fit a definition.

When I arrived at the Betty Ford Center in 2004 seeking treatment for my addiction to Adderall, I was given a copy of what is commonly known as the Big Book of Alcoholics Anonymous. This text strictly refers to "alcohol," but I was advised to focus on the behaviors and feelings it described and not to get hung up on the words. In recovery, we refer to this as identifying in—looking for commonalities between yourself and others to remind yourself that you're in the right place. The opposite is called identifying out—looking for reasons you don't belong. A person who identifies out may hear a story about someone who drinks whisky, but as a wine drinker, they focus on this as a way to build a case for why they shouldn't be in treatment or meetings.

Similarly, I regularly refer to your child but this is not specifically meant to refer only to young people. I have led interventions for people in their mid-sixties whose parents hired me. Regardless of your child's age—whether they be 17, 33 or 52 or older—this book pertains to them. The techniques discussed here can appropriately be applied to any family member, friend or loved one suffering from addiction.

Perhaps you have gone months or even years kicking the can down the road thinking your son or daughter will improve without any professional help or intervention—only to find temporary improvements followed by relapses. The wait-and-see position has likely only led you to more disappointment. While it's not impossible your child will seek professional help themselves, such actions usually take place only after years of drinking and using drugs followed by some devastating event, like being incarcerated, injured in an accident or nearly escaping a fatal overdose. The wait-and-see attitude seldom yields satisfactory results.

The stories I hear from parents often detail long histories of their children's addiction, often starting in the teenage years and coming to light as a result of troubles at school. Some teenagers can maintain good enough grades to get them into college, where once they're out of their parents' purview, they either decide to stop partying or become more entrenched in drug and alcohol culture. Though some kids can hold themselves together even through college thanks to their youth and good health, that often changes after graduating—when they can no longer sleep in late and take afternoon classes.

Drug and alcohol addiction is not always a flashing neon sign. It is usually much subtler and easily hidden from strangers. Most addicts are not reduced to living under bridges in filthy clothes, although these cases exist as well. Many are well-educated, well-dressed, smart and talented people who can hide their addiction from their acquaintances. This charade usually begins to fail eventually, thus revealing the reality of their situation.

Sometimes their addiction is driven by undiagnosed and untreated depression, anxiety or trauma. Many parents hang on to the hope that simple therapy or medication will solve all their child's problems rather than admitting they're an addict. Addiction can present like other mental health problems, but it's necessary to start treating the addiction first before understanding the addiction's root causes. I liken it to a beautiful mosaic floor covered in years of ground-in dirt; until the floor is fully clean, there's no way to tell what will be revealed underneath.

Despite the possibility of additional diagnoses, drugs and alcohol are usually the cause of most of an addict's problems. This is important to understand— once a person has become *addicted* to drugs and alcohol, there's no going back. Addicts and alcoholics can never return to recreational drinking or smoking. It is a bell that can never be unrung.

Prior to getting sober, I lived in a persistent state of depression and anxiety which was greatly reduced when I stopped using prescription pills and drinking every day. This is not to say sobriety has fully cured my depression and anxiety. Even so, being sober has made a tremendous difference in my life. While there are times I still feel depressed or anxious, these feelings are no longer debilitating. Through recovery, I've learned skills to help me work through these feelings in a healthy and productive way. Whereas symptoms of depression and anxiety used to put me on my ass for days, I'm now able to re-center myself within 30 minutes or a couple of hours.

Having been in recovery for many years, I've realized that most of my problems are self-imposed—examples of this are catastrophizing future events that may never occur, or which end up being much less harrowing than I imagine them to be. Problems like this usually stem from a lack of spiritual maintenance and can often be relieved by connecting with other recovering addicts, resting, exercising, eating properly, praying and meditating. There is a well-known acronym in addiction recovery called HALT, which stands for Hungry, Angry, Lonely and Tired. It's a checklist people in recovery can run through before making any hurried decisions like quitting a job or ending a relationship. Once they're in treatment, these skills will be at your son or daughter's disposal.

Doing an intervention is not complicated, nor does it involve a secret process that only professional interventionists are taught. Still, there is a significant amount of information you need to have before attempting one yourself, and the logistics need to be well-managed in order to achieve a successful outcome.

Interventions are commonly used to compel people to accept treatment for life-threatening addictions to drugs, alcohol and food, as well as for process addictions to things like sex, technology, gambling and shopping (sometimes referred to as "debting"). These programs often involve treatment for mental illness as well.

The strategies outlined in this book will provide you with the information necessary to conduct a successful intervention for your son or daughter, regardless of their age or drug of choice. With that in mind, let's get started.

Understanding Addiction

**"Addiction is a potentially fatal illness, but
it is also eminently recoverable."
-Dr. Kevin McCauley**

One of my responsibilities as a professional interventionist is to educate families about addiction. It's important for my clients to know addiction is a life-threatening brain disease which has the ability to rewire the human brain and cause people to behave irrationally and dangerously. A person in active addiction may drive under the influence of drugs or alcohol endangering themselves and other people or steal money from a parent or spouse. The same person sober might never engage in such risky behavior or act in a manner that contradicts their values.

In active addiction a person may choose to continue using drugs and be homeless instead of getting sober and living safely in their parents' or family's home. They may forgo eating regularly and go into dangerous neighborhoods to buy drugs instead of doing the work it requires to stay clean and pursue their dreams of becoming a professional radio announcer or raising a family. Under the spell of addiction, getting high is their top priority and it will trump everything else in their life. It can even mean prostituting themselves for drug money or leaving their young child unattended while they meet their dealer.

Any parent or family member of an active or recovering addict knows what it's like living with a person who's responsible one minute and dangerous the next. Routine responsibilities like running to the supermarket or being on time for a special event are often difficult challenges for a person in the midst of their disease. Instead of coming straight home from the supermarket, they might disappear for days on end. Instead of them showing up to events on time, you might get a call from the police that they're being held for driving while intoxicated or for possession and trespassing.

For some parents, these examples may seem far-fetched because their son or daughter's addictions have not yet reached a point of desperation. For others, it's an accurate description of their current circumstances. Still, my point here is to make clear how powerful addiction can be and why it can cause your child to behave in upsetting and dangerous ways.

Contrary to some generalizations, addicts are not bad people even if they sometimes do bad things after they come in contact with drugs. In fact, addicts may be driven into addiction as a result of underlying trauma or feelings of shame, which is important to understand. Shame and guilt are very different emotions. Guilt is feeling badly for doing a specific behavior, like stealing money from a friend's wallet. Shame is feeling like you are at heart a bad person.

While a person in addiction may not feel guilt for doing "bad" things to survive and sustain their addiction, underneath that, they may feel extreme shame about themselves—and the things a person does during addiction can compound those feelings of shame. Shame alone can drive a person to drink, but experiencing shame is not proof of a person's character.

In fact, addicts can be quite sensitive and easily hurt, which may in part explain why they are addicted to mood-altering substances. Leading up to taking my first drug, I had a long history of feeling badly about myself due to low self-esteem, self-doubt, depression and loneliness. Feeling the effects of that first drug made all those feelings melt away. I remember thinking I had finally found what I'd been looking for my entire life.

Discovering amphetamines marked a life changing event in my life. The drugs tricked me into believing I was having a normal human experience. I described my response to Ritalin and then Adderall as not being able to see and then being given glasses. At the time, I believed the transformation was miraculous. Looking back on this period of my life however, it's clear that getting high was only relieving me of negative feelings. In the beginning, drugs produce desirable outcomes for people prone to addiction. As a result it's easy to understand why addicts continuously seek to recreate the experience.

Ultimately, it becomes increasingly harder to chase that feeling of comfort and safety, and it requires more substances to get the same experience. In the beginning, one or two drinks may be sufficient to achieve the desired result, but over time, that number can grow exponentially. This type of progression is true for all drugs. In late stage alcoholism, there may be no amount of drinks which can produce the desired effect—the drug may stop working altogether. On the other hand, sometimes a person can become completely intoxicated after only one drink.

For many addicted people, addiction is the result of seeking a short-term solution to their problems. Taking a drink or using drugs makes them feel better about themselves, but addiction is progressive. Soon one drink or one joint isn't enough to produce the same feeling of escape, and more drugs are needed to achieve the same result. This pattern continues, snowballing until the addict has lost the power of choice and getting high is no longer an option—it becomes an all-consuming, full-time job.

The disease theory of addiction identifies drug-seeking behavior as compulsive rather than a conscious choice due to chemical changes in the brain that happen with regular substance abuse. The National Institute on Drug Abuse (NIDA) compares addiction to other medical diseases, such as heart disease and diabetes.

In simple terms, the addicted brain prioritizes drug use as being more important than other human needs; things such as eating, personal safety, self-care and obtaining shelter become subordinate to getting and using drugs.

In active addiction, your son or daughter is not the same person you once drove to baseball practice or took to piano lessons. Persistent drug use has reprogrammed their brain to feed their addiction at any cost—which can include lying and stealing. In some cases, it can mean prostituting themselves, cheating or breaking the law. In active addiction, it becomes nearly impossible for someone to disobey their brain's directive to use drugs.

I first heard about the disease model of addiction during a lecture in 2004 when I was in treatment at the Betty Ford Center. The lecturer, a former Navy flight surgeon turned morphine addict, said the diseased brain sends the user urgent messages like, "If you don't get me drugs, really bad things are going to happen—and you may even die." I remember hearing that and knowing it was true from my own experience. If I had applied the same focus and urgency to my career in commercial real estate, I would have made a lot of money.

Once a person has been taken hostage by their addiction, reasonable arguments are no longer effective in influencing their behavior and it becomes necessary to stage an intervention. An intervention is an orchestrated attempt to penetrate a person's preoccupation with substances long enough for them to see the real effects of their disease. Our objective is to raise a reasonable level of doubt about them continuing to use drugs and offer them a glimpse of the possibilities of life in sobriety. Their willingness to accept treatment may be subtle and hard to read, or it may be open and enthusiastic once your child has surrendered and let down their guard.

By the time I was intervened on and agreed to accept treatment, I was powerless over my addictions. As described in the first step of Alcoholics Anonymous, my life had become unmanageable. The time I discovered amphetamines to the time I arrived at the Betty Ford Center was 10 years almost to the day.

At the time, I had been seeing a psychiatrist who died unexpectedly while vacationing on Cape Cod, leaving me cut off from a steady supply of hard to get Schedule II prescriptions. Not having a reliable source meant I had to begin doctor shopping to keep up with my demand for more drugs—and doctor shopping is an onerous task that requires a tremendous amount of time and money, leaving little time for work or family.

A lot of doctors I saw would begrudgingly accommodate me one time, but made sure I knew not to come back in the future. Some doctors made me sign a letter attesting that I was not doctor shopping, which I easily did without reservation. This was right around the time when walk-in clinics were starting to appear, which made it easier because I could show up without an appointment. Some of the doctors didn't seem to care if I was shopping, or they weren't aware they were one of many in my steady rotation of prescribers.

Somewhere towards the end of bouncing from one doctor to the next, I found another psychiatrist I felt comfortable confiding in and who knew I was doctor shopping. He tried talking to me about getting help, but I couldn't imagine surviving without Adderall. I thought being sober meant having to live in a constant state of withdrawal, which for me produced flu-like symptoms and would cause me to fall asleep every time I sat down. Being out of drugs also caused debilitating anxiety and panic attacks that sometimes landed me in the emergency room on a Benadryl drip. At the end I was no longer attempting to get high; I was merely trying to function.

Codependency and Enabling

Codependency is a behavioral condition in a relationship where one person enables another person's addiction, poor mental health, immaturity, irresponsibility or under-achievement. Among the core characteristics of codependency is an excessive reliance on other people for approval and a sense of identity. It's typical for parents and children to have codependent relationships, especially when addiction is involved.

Consider the origins of how the parent-child relationship begins through innocent acts of love. Every parent remembers their newborn son or daughter crying for their mother or father to comfort them because they were hungry, needed to be changed or were experiencing discomfort or an unfamiliar emotion. In response, the parents rush into their child's nursery to try and make everything better for them. Not coming to their child's aid would feel cruel and might make them feel like a bad or unloving parent.

More experienced parents with the advantage of hindsight, along with professional caregivers such as nurses and nannies, may advise the parents to refrain from snapping to attention every time their baby cries. They counsel parents to let their children cry for a short time so they can learn to comfort themselves. Even though this makes good sense, it's difficult for parents to resist the urge to take action at the first sound their newborn makes. According to research, human beings are genetically programmed to respond to the sound of a crying baby:

The very specific sound qualities of screaming set off the amygdala, or the region of the brain that generates a fear response. This helps explain our very physical response to babies fussing: racing heartbeat, rising blood pressure, twinges of panic or discomfort.

Of course, being a responsive parent doesn't mean your newborn will need a spot in rehab 18 years later. Even so, this illustrates how parent-child codependency can begin. By way of this example, you can see as a parent how you may be affected when your son or daughter is expelled from school, or when they get arrested for drinking and driving as an adult. Your natural reaction may be to save them from distress and shield them from consequences. Furthermore, you may blame yourself for being an imperfect parent and hold yourself responsible for your child's behavior…even though they're 34 years old.

Conversely, you may be the type of person who has their parenting down from the very beginning. You didn't take any crap and you weren't afraid to impose consequences or set healthy boundaries—yet somehow, your child still struggles with an addiction to drugs or alcohol. The diseases of addiction and mental illness are not parallel to environmental influences or conventional thinking, so trying to understand how these diseases developed may not make sense to you. In these situations, parents are left with an unpleasant mental choice to make.

No parent wants to admit their son or daughter is somehow defective, so instead, they begin blaming themselves for their children's problems. At the same time, addicted children—regardless of their age—are highly skilled manipulators who are very good at turning the spotlight away from themselves and blaming others for their problems.

If your son or daughter is successful in convincing you the problem is, for example, your extensive work schedule or bad parenting and not their addiction, they will have essentially negotiated a free pass to keep using drugs while you steep in guilt. The more you blame yourself, the freer they are to continue their behavior. Once you cut through your guilt and start focusing on their addiction, they may even threaten violence, self-harm or suicide. I've had numerous parents tell me their son or daughter threatened to commit suicide if they were to be sent to treatment— and nothing stops a parent faster than the thought of their child dying because of something they did.

Threatening suicide is sometimes used as a manipulate tactic intended to help addicts evade treatment; however, such threats must always be taken seriously as sometimes addicted people do become hopeless and take their own lives. If you have any serious concerns about your son or daughter's welfare, do not hesitate to take them to the hospital to be evaluated by a psychiatrist or other qualified professional.

For my part, I have personally struggled with codependency and have tremendous empathy for what addicted families go through. At times I've allowed myself to wrongly believe if I were a better person, other people would be happier. These thoughts usually manifested themselves in misguided ideas about financial insecurity. For example, if I'd made more money, my wife would be a happier person or my teenage daughter would be better adjusted. While having more money does allow people to enjoy more things, it has little effect on someone's overall happiness.

On a particularly bad day in treatment and after being thrown out of the family program, I was later intervened on by the counselor who demanded I leave the group earlier. He looked at me with incredible frankness. "You're so codependent," he said. "You may need Al-Anon as much as you need Alcoholics Anonymous (AA), because you think everything is your fault," he said.

For those who don't know, Al-Anon is a sister program to Alcoholics Anonymous which helps people recover from codependency. Hearing my counselor suggest it shed light on an entirely separate category of behaviors, behaviors which were perhaps the genesis of my addictions. As I thought it over, a lot of my behaviors and feelings of inadequacy were driven by my need to have other people's approval. After months of self-exploration, I finally concluded that no one other than me would ever be able to give the approval I needed to feel okay about myself.

The same counselor had previously given an important talk to the patients. The concept he explained was that in every relationship, there's a "bad" person who embodies shame and a "good" person who embodies shamelessness. For his part, the counselor described his relationship with his first wife. He explained that when he woke up in the morning, he would look at his wife and if she looked happy, he knew it was going to be a good day. If she looked unhappy, it was going to be a bad day. I recognized myself in these statements because they described how I often felt in my relationships.

While some of these examples are aimed at couples, similar dynamics exist in parent-child relationships. I'm sure anyone reading this can identify with having to tip toe around your own home because you're afraid to set off your volatile son or daughter. The adage that you're only as happy as your least happy child is nowhere more true than for parents struggling with an addicted child.

Codependency and enabling are most evident in how parents fail to follow through on consequences after a violation. For example, you tell your son or daughter to be home by 11 pm for their curfew and when they saunter in at 1 am, the behavior either goes unpunished or receives nothing more than a verbal warning, thus causing them to push the boundary further next time. Not enforcing the rules is enabling, because it enables your child to repeat bad behavior. Don't beat yourself up if this example hits close to home—it describes most families struggling with drug and alcohol addiction or dysfunction.

In some cases, I have seen mothers and fathers become as sick as their drug-addicted children—even exhibiting the same irrational behaviors. I recently worked with a mother who resigned from her job as a successful executive to manage her son's addictions only to watch them get worse. The afternoon I brought this woman's son to treatment, she called me in tears saying she was so scared and maybe sending him to treatment was a mistake. Having worked with this mother for several months, I felt comfortable raising my voice and saying: "Are you kidding me? Tonight should be the best night's sleep you've ever had! Your son is finally in a safe place and you don't have to be up all night worrying about him."

A few days later, the same mother called me and I could hear in her voice she had been sleeping very well. Six weeks into her son's treatment, she sounded like an entirely different person.

Parents are notoriously complicit in their children's addiction. Almost every mother who contacts me feels compelled to begin the conversation by highlighting her son's intelligence, explaining why he's too smart for treatment or AA meetings, how he went to one AA meeting and didn't like it or how he felt the crowd at AA meetings was somehow beneath him. I usually allow these parents some latitude for sharing this information and then start educating them about the real nature of addiction and how it destroys all lives equally regardless of a person's socioeconomic status. The disease does not care who attended the best universities or who had the most successful practice. Addiction strips away labels and equalizes everyone it affects.

I was recently contacted by the mother of a 38-year-old man who had failed out of every treatment center he'd attended from Pennsylvania to California. He was still living in her home using drugs and not working. After listening to her explain at length about her son's multiple failed treatment attempts, I suggested sending him to treatment in Israel to keep him from leaving treatment prematurely since he had exhausted so many good treatment options in the United States. "Going overseas isn't an option because he has a girlfriend," she retorted.

By the mother's comment, I knew what was causing her son to stay stuck in this cycle of treatment and relapse. Often enough, codependents and enablers are each getting something unhealthy from the relationship. For instance, a father who aids his daughter getting drugs by giving her money may enjoy the love and approval she provides him in return. The father may fool himself into believing the money is to purchase clothes or food, but he ultimately knows the truth. This isn't representative of every parent with an addicted son or daughter, but it is fairly common.

Addiction is a family disease. Treating an addicted family member without exploring the family system significantly reduces the chances of long-term recovery. Families who lack this awareness often see addiction as an individual problem and will say things like, "Robert is the alcoholic, so why do *I* have to go to Al-Anon meetings?" They're often surprised to learn what is required of them as a recovering family.

During a pre-intervention meeting with the mother and father of an adult addict, I was met with surprising resistance telling them that they would need to participate in the treatment center's five-day family program. "I can't go to the family program because I have to work," the father exclaimed. I asked the father if the family ever went on vacations. "Of course," he said. "Then this is your vacation," I replied. Needless to say, this was not the family's first intervention or their first time sending their son to treatment.

Regardless of what your experience has been with your son or daughter in the past, intervention and treatment is your opportunity to reconsider what you want the relationship to look like going forward. If you were codependent and enabling in the past, it doesn't mean you have to continue that parenting style in the future. You can use this time to understand the importance of creating structure and setting boundaries, no matter their age.

ONE

Preparations for Intervention

Getting Started

Having worked with many families, I can imagine you are anxious to get started. However, rushed or improvised interventions are rarely successful because they tend to skip the careful planning and preparation professional interventionists focus on. Fortunately, these are mistakes I've learned to avoid with experience.

At the very beginning of my career, I got a call from a woman asking me to lead a last-minute intervention for her 40-year-old husband who was addicted to painkillers. She called me in the morning and wanted me to do the intervention that afternoon. She said it was an emergency because her husband's older brother was in town overnight, and if we didn't do it right away, we would miss our chance of getting her husband into treatment.

I had just gotten my certification as an interventionist and was eager to start building my practice. At that time, I would never have considered turning down a new client. When I arrived at the woman's chaotic home a few hours later, I immediately felt apprehensive as I stood there watching her argue with her husband's mother and brother. It was nearly impossible to get them to sit down long enough to discuss a strategy or write their impact letters, both of which are vital means of communication used in interventions and which should be completed well in advance.

When the woman's husband walked through the door, he knew exactly what was about to unfold and turned into a raging maniac. Neither his mother or brother were willing to confront him after seeing him so angry. Meanwhile, the woman sat on the coach hurling accusations at her husband, further fueling his anger. I did everything I could to gain control over the situation, but that only made me the object of his frustration. I knew our chances of having a successful intervention were already in steep decline.

It was clear to me the woman's husband was an addict and needed treatment, but because the intervention was thrown together so hastily, it failed to reach any successful outcome. After two hours of listening to him scream and deny accusations of being addicted to painkillers, the husband stood up and walked out. A few minutes later, the wife announced she had to pick up her daughter from aftercare and walked out as well.

Later that evening, I called the wife to see if she

was following up with any of the consequences she'd threatened her husband with. Instead, I found out the entire family, including the husband, were out to dinner celebrating someone's birthday. I was disappointed. "If you enacted any of the consequences we discussed," I told her, "your husband would be going to treatment tonight or tomorrow morning." She thanked me for calling and hung up.

The following morning at 6 am, I received a menacing phone call from the husband threatening me to return the money his mother paid me for the intervention. After listening to his threats for 15 minutes, I agreed to return the money in full. I tried reaching out to him a few times afterwards to offer support or take him to an AA or Narcotics Anonymous meeting. He never responded, and I never heard from his wife again either.

The encounter made me realize my experience up until that point had primarily been limited to addicts and alcoholics in recovery—people who were willingly abstaining from drugs and alcohol. On the other hand, treatment-resistant individuals would do almost anything to avoid getting help and keep drinking and using drugs—a completely different scenario than the classroom experience and mock training I'd received. Nothing could replace the real-life experience I would gain over the next several years working with families in crisis.

In hindsight, that first intervention is one of the most valued learning experiences of my career because it taught me three essential lessons:

1. There are no easy interventions.
2. Proper preparation increases the chances of a successful outcome.
3. Providing a safe and non-confrontational environment for the addicted person improves cooperation and success.

As an experienced interventionist, I am thorough in my preparation and deliberate in my process leading up to an intervention. I interview everyone who intends to participate in the intervention, oversee and coordinate logistics, schedule sufficient time to prepare the participants, work through an extensive list of excuses the individual may use to get out of going to treatment and spend time discussing the feelings of apprehension anyone may feel prior to the intervention. Sometimes, I even role play as a belligerent addict so everyone knows the worst of what to expect.

I'm candid with families about the challenges interventions present as well as the challenges that come after treatment. Getting their son or daughter into a program is a victory, but it only marks the beginning of a much longer process. I never want to be caught in a situation where I neglected to properly advise a family. I want them to know their child could leave treatment against medical advice, or that they need to be escorted from residential treatment to sober living because there's a chance they won't make it past the airport bar or nearest liquor store sober.

As we begin this journey, there are some general principles to keep in mind.

Take Care with Timing

Interventions should not be rushed unless the individual is in police custody or in the hospital. In other words, only in situations where there is a short window of opportunity to leverage a unique situation. If your child has been arrested and asks you to bail them out, only do so if they'll agree to be transferred directly to treatment upon release. That means no stopping at home to pick up anything, not even for medications or to pack a bag. If they're in the hospital because of an accidental overdose or having been involved in an accident, they may recognize their own vulnerability and be willing to accept treatment—but the same rules apply. They must be taken to treatment with no stops (there will be more about this later).

Similarly, the intervention should not be delayed if your son or daughter has pending police charges or is on probation. Any decisions involving the possibility of legal consequences should be discussed with your child's attorney; however, I've found courts and probation officers to be cooperative when someone is seeking professional help for addiction. Even so, they will want confirmation from the treatment center and the ability to communicate with your child regularly. I've heard many probation officers say this in their own words: "As long as I know they're in treatment, there's no problem."

This can be an additional form of leverage if your son or daughter gets restless in treatment and threatens to leave. The treatment team can remind them if they leave treatment, the probation officer will be notified and will most likely issue a warrant for their arrest. Knowing this will hopefully keep them from taking off.

If your son or daughter is drinking or using drugs as they usually do, take the necessary time to prepare a carefully engineered intervention that is most likely to produce a successful outcome. Carry on expeditiously to avoid the possibility of them overdosing, getting arrested or hurting themselves or another person. In other words, move as quickly as possible without sacrificing any necessary preparation.

Another important consideration is your son or daughter's age. If they are nearing the age of majority, which in most US states is 18 years old, and you have been contemplating getting them professional help for a substance use disorder or mental illness, act while the law is still in your favor.

While your son or daughter is a minor, you have certain legal rights such as speaking with their treatment team without obtaining their permission and making treatment decisions on their behalf. If they are legally an adult, you no longer have these privileges and must rely on them to be cooperative. Having an uncooperative adult child in treatment or who needs treatment sometimes leads parents to seek guardianship, which is a complicated and expensive legal process.

Having your hands tied is frustrating because even though your son or daughter is legally an adult, their behavior can be that of a young teenager. This is to be expected—people who are addicted to substances often fail to mature at the same rate as their peers, leaving them incapable of making good decisions.

Every Intervention is Unique

When a parent contacts me about leading an intervention for their son or daughter, I automatically start creating a mental blueprint of what the intervention will look like. I want to have a clear idea of what the situation involves so I can properly advise them. Some of the questions I want to understand are:

- Does the family have the emotional wherewithal to see this to completion?
- What is the relationship between the parents and the child?
- Regardless of age, is the child financially dependent on his or her parents?
- What is the familial status (i.e. are the parents together, is the person in question married, do they have children)?
- What is their past treatment history?

It's important for me to assess each situation and determine how quickly I can move forward with each family. Some families require a lot of preparation because there's years of codependency and enabling that has to be worked through. Other families are calmer and less emotional about the process and move quickly. It's always important to move quickly, but rushing an intervention with an unprepared family can result in the individual not going to treatment, which creates more problems for the family down the road.

Every intervention presents unique challenges and circumstances that must be considered carefully before moving forward. Carrying out an intervention without professional assistance will present its own greater challenges, as you will see later, though it also offers some unique opportunities. After all, parents often understand the complexities of a family system better than anyone else and always have the child's best interest at heart.

Regardless of how difficult your son or daughter's problems may be, there is no reason why they can't recover from addiction and go on to be as happy and accomplished as any other person. In the years I've been sober, I've met other recovering addicts with successful careers in medicine, politics, law, business and the arts. More importantly, these people have successful home lives as well. In sobriety, they got married, had children, traveled to foreign places and accomplished life-long dreams.

Provided they are willing to do the work to stay sober, there's no reason your son or daughter can't accomplish their goals.

Don't Blame Yourself

It's common for parents to blame themselves for their children's alcohol or drug addictions. Perhaps you're asking what you did wrong or thinking that if you were a better parent, this wouldn't be happening. Maybe if you had more money (or less money) or sent them to a better school (or a less-competitive school), you wouldn't be here today. The details are unimportant—I have seen kids become addicted whose parents showed them endless love and attention and who attended the best private schools.

When my daughter was born, I knew the only thing I could do with certainty was to love her. The rest of the time, I would be making decisions on the fly. There are a lot of things I could have done better —for instance, I could have been more present and less distracted by technology. More importantly, I didn't get sober until after her second birthday. I'm sure there are plenty of things you would have done differently too, but you wouldn't be reading this book if you didn't have an endless well of love for your child.

Doing Your Own Intervention Is a Risk

While I'm going to give you all of the necessary information to successfully intervene for your son or daughter, I would be remiss if I didn't tell you the challenges one faces without a professional interventionist.

On the day your child walks in the room and sits on the couch, you must be able to detach from them in order to achieve a successful outcome. Even if you choose a third person to lead the intervention (more about this later), you must not "rescue" your son or daughter from getting help, no matter how much it pains you to hear them beg not to send them and swear they will change. If you rescue them or lose your determination, you will have effectively granted them permission to keep drinking or using drugs indefinitely. A misstep like this could take years to repair and cause an untold amount of damage.

If your son or daughter has a history of harming themselves or has previously attempted suicide, I *urge* you to think twice about performing your own intervention. Interventionists are experienced practitioners who follow a standard of care similar to the Hippocratic oath: "Do no harm." Taking the responsibility of performing your own intervention means the same standard applies to you.

It's imperative to approach your intervention as earnestly as you would any other life-threatening illness like cancer. There are no acceptable half-results when it comes to performing an intervention. The day does not end until your son or daughter has been safely admitted into treatment.

Before getting into the mechanics of running an intervention, it's important that you understand how the persistent use of addictive substances alters the human brain and causes people to act in unacceptable and dangerous ways. Secondly, it's also important for you to know how your relationship with your son or daughter unintentionally contributes to their addiction problems. To that end, the first two chapters of this book will cover understanding addiction, codependency and enabling.

According to the National Institute on Drug Abuse, there were nearly 138,000 combined drug-related deaths in the United States in 2017 and 2018. Additionally, most people use drugs for the first time when they are teenagers. To avoid the worst outcomes, it's important to act as early as possible.

Making the decision to intervene on behalf of your son or daughter to help them recover from addiction is a courageous act of love, and I admire you for taking the first step of a long journey. As you are about to see, putting together an intervention is hard work.

First Steps

Hosting a successful intervention is in many ways like hosting any other special event like a wedding or a Bar Mitzvah. It requires having a clearly stated goal, making a plan that will result in achieving that goal, staying organized and sticking to the plan. Here, the goal is to get your son or daughter into treatment so they may begin recovering from their addiction and mental illness and go on to live a long, happy and prosperous life.

Begin by getting a notebook and sectioning it off into categories to keep important notes and contact information you can easily refer to later. Some of the categories you will need are listed below though you may add additional categories along the way. You may also want to distribute some information to the intervention participants, such as the address and time of the intervention, hotel information, restaurant information and anything else you think may be important for them to have. Here is some information I track carefully:

- Participants and their contact information
- Insurance information, such as member ID number and telephone numbers
- Treatment programs and contact people
- Pre-intervention agenda
- Intervention agenda
- Flight information (plus contact information for the person meeting them at the airport)
- Payments and out-of-pocket expenses (eg, insurance copays)
- Impact letters
- Timeline of addiction history (eg, arrests, job terminations)
- Venues

Set aside a block of uninterrupted time that you can speak freely on the telephone without your son or daughter overhearing you or being interrupted by something else. I like making sensitive calls while sitting in my parked car, because it gives me privacy and the ability to take notes while using the car's speakerphone.

Scheduling and Logistics

Scheduling and managing logistics are important considerations in hosting a successful intervention as well. The first step is to confirm a date for the pre-intervention meeting and the intervention itself, and to start building the itinerary around these two days.

Similar to planning a wedding, having a specific date will set the pace for how quickly you will have to work and creates an official timeline that everything must revolve around.

If the intervention requires key participants to travel, allow sufficient time for that. Select an appropriately located hotel and make sure everybody stays at the same place. Anytime you can eliminate moving parts, the better off you are. Having participants at multiple hotels will make things more difficult. Select an appropriately-priced hotel near where the intervention will be held and explain to everyone involved that that's where they'll be staying. Don't get caught up in other people's drama around their personal preferences. I've seen family members refuse to stay at the same hotel as others because "cousin Sarah always gets her way." Stay focused!

Don't hold up the intervention because of one person's schedule unless that person is a parent, spouse or significant other, or any person the individual needs present to accept treatment. For example, it's unlikely your adult son is going to accept treatment if his wife is not involved in the process. Even so, there are cases where excluding a spouse may be necessary because of their own addiction problems or for fear of them sabotaging the intervention.

I recently led an intervention for an adult where a group decision was made to exclude the individual's parents from participating because they didn't believe their son required treatment for his alcoholism. In that case, I spoke with the parents a number of times only to have them rebuke the idea of sending their son to treatment. Once the intervention was completed, the son notified his parents and luckily, they were willing to be cooperative. Regardless of people's busy schedules, participants should treat the intervention like any medical emergency and prioritize being there.

Something to consider: I once participated in an intervention where the addict refused to accept treatment until he received permission from his girlfriend. The girlfriend wasn't initially invited to participate in the intervention because the family didn't think she would be a factor in his decision to accept treatment. The man's family didn't know the relationship was as serious as it was (or didn't want to believe it was), and wasn't sure she would be cooperative. In the end, the girlfriend supported him going to treatment, but who knows if that support was because the man was given an ultimatum or because she sincerely agreed.

When I see someone struggling to accept treatment during an intervention, I sometimes ask them if there is anyone not present they can confer with, someone they trust who has helped them make important decisions in the past. That person can be a romantic interest the family isn't aware of, a therapist, work friend or anyone else their individual considers a confidant. Sometimes, this can push an intervention over the edge to success.

You will need to allow time for a pre-intervention meeting the day before the actual intervention, which will require everybody participating the next day to be present. With the pre-intervention and intervention dates set, you'll need to start focusing on the remaining logistics, which include:

- Inviting and screening participants
- Confirming insurance benefits (in-network vs. out-of-network)
- Selecting a treatment program
- Creating an agenda for the pre-intervention and intervention
- Arranging transportation to treatment
- Payment arrangements for out-of-pocket expenses
- Writing impact letters (prior to the pre-intervention)
- Discussing and implementing consequences
- Selecting an intervention venue
- Getting help for yourself and other family members

These steps are written here roughly in the order they should be handled. You may be going into this process already knowing which program your son or daughter is going to attend or who will participate in the intervention.

The pre-intervention and intervention are best scheduled back-to-back. For example, if the pre-intervention is on Thursday, have the intervention take place on Friday morning. The pre-intervention meeting is a dress rehearsal, so you want it to be fresh in everyone's mind the following morning. The participants may be anxious to get on with the real thing, so there's no benefit in putting it off. After all, any unnecessary delays just create additional risk of the intervention not happening.

Ask the participants to keep their schedules open during these two days. Having people show up late or get anxious because they have other commitments is distracting and possibly damaging. If someone can't commit to full participation, it may be better to ask them to write an impact letter that can be read on their behalf at the intervention instead.

The actual intervention starts the minute the individual enters the room and doesn't end until they agree to accept treatment. In general, they shouldn't go longer than two hours at most. Participants should remain in place until the individual is safely on their way to treatment. If the intervention party disperses too quickly and the individual retracts their decision to accept treatment, you could be left doing another intervention by yourself.

Your friends and family participating in the intervention are your support system and are an important part of achieving a successful outcome. When leading an intervention, I don't consider my day over until the addict has been admitted into treatment, and even then, I have received phone calls from treatment facilities later the same night saying the person wants to leave.

It is best to remove expectations of the intervention proceeding as planned; allow the process to unfold naturally. It's not possible to control everything —once the intervention begins, it's too late to dwell on details you may have missed or what you should have done differently. In other words, learn to roll with the punches. If, for example, you planned to have your son or daughter on the 1 pm flight but instead have to take the 3 or 5 pm flight because they hijacked the intervention for two hours, learn to accept the situation.

Do everything you can to plan a successful intervention, but don't become overly stressed in trying to control everything. By being too controlling, the chances of a successful outcome start diminishing. There is a spiritual component to interventions, and part of that spirituality is allowing the day to unfold without forcing the pieces. I can tell you this: the tighter you hold reins, the more likely it is of going off the rails.

On a personal note, I have led interventions that began early in the morning and ended 1,000 miles away, 14 hours later. On the other hand, I have had cases where the intervention was finished by early afternoon with the individual in a local treatment center. Perfectly executed interventions don't happen all the time, even for professionals. The end goal is getting your son or daughter into treatment so they can get professional help for their addiction and or mental health problems. If this happens, the intervention went perfectly.

Inviting and Screening Participants

Deciding who to invite and who not to invite to the intervention are decisions worthy of important consideration. Some families have a lot of options on who to invite to participate, while others don't due to lost or damaged relationships as a result of your son or daughter's addictions.

I worked with a family that insisted their father's best friend from college be at his intervention. They said their father respected this friend and would not want to disappoint him by not accepting treatment per his advice. However, when I reached out to the friend, he was unenthusiastic about the relationship because the father had treated him badly—even taking advantage of him when they worked together. The friend ultimately decided to attend the intervention because he wanted to help the family rather than harbor resentment. Still, other scorned friends may not be as gracious as this person was.

There are plenty of stories like this because people who abuse alcohol and drugs can become selfish and self-centered. Often, there are scorned ex-boyfriends and girlfriends who have been cheated on or unceremoniously dumped because the addict chose drugs over the relationship. Many times, people in the throes of addiction fail to carry out their responsibilities or show up for things because they're drinking or using. I know this from experience.

When I was addicted, I would often fail to show up for work meetings or personal obligations because of debilitating anxiety. I was regularly awake in the middle of the night making things, exploring the internet or taking high doses of Adderall. I would finally get into bed at 3 or 4 am only to be awakened by the alarm a few hours later. I was physically and mentally exhausted and rarely in fit condition. I did everything I could to keep up appearances and blame my lack of sleep on having "a lot on my mind."

One such morning, I was invited to attend the Bat Mitzvah of my good friend's daughter. I woke up in a panic and plied myself with black coffee and food from the corner deli. I had no idea where the Bat Mitzvah was being held and I was already an hour late. I had cut myself shaving, my suit was tight because I was always continuously getting fatter and my breathing was labored. I finally called my friend's mobile saying I couldn't make it that morning but would attend the party later that evening. My life was completely unmanageable. I felt guilty for missing the Bat Mitzvah and shame for being such a bad friend. That morning was not unique—most of my mornings were like that one.

It's not unusual for me to receive calls from parents describing critical situations like overdoses and arrests. Still, I'm confounded when parents choose to take a "wait and see" position. One mother contacted me several times to address what she described as an urgent matter, and then quickly changed tack and decided not to take action until her son's pending charges for possession and trespassing were dropped. I advised her that delaying the intervention and getting her son into treatment was dangerous because he could have a fatal overdose, be arrested again, or hurt himself or somebody in the time it took to resolve legal issues. Unfortunately, these reactions are all too common.

How Many People Should Come to an Intervention?

Don't be overly concerned if the number of willing participants in an intervention is limited to a handful of people—this doesn't mean you will be unsuccessful. I have successfully completed interventions with only the mother and father present before, though having a larger group of participants (up to a point) is theoretically better if they all add value to the process. Still, including people without significant influence or who aren't genuinely invested in an intervention will ultimately be counterproductive.

As mentioned, I've had situations where an important figure, such as a parent or spouse, was excluded because they posed a threat to the success of the intervention. The reasons for excluding someone major are usually that their interests are not aligned with the intervention, or they don't want to see the person recover because it will take something away from them (eg. A sibling will no longer be the favorite child, or a parent will no longer be able to blame the addict for their own misfortunes). Other reasons include not trusting the participant to be sober at the intervention, or because their relationship is too contentious and will be distracting to manage for the interventionist.

In family systems that have been affected by addiction, every person plays a contributing role as if they were characters in a play. While you may not believe it, sometime the "characters" in these dramas believe they stand to benefit from maintaining the status quo. They may be addicted to the emotional drama and crave the stimulation, or perhaps they think the addict's behavior keeps the attention off their own flaws.

When families hire me to lead interventions, I screen all prospective participants to help determine if anybody should be eliminated. It's unusual for me to suggest someone be removed, but through the screening process, I often learn things the family members may have missed that warrant further discussion. While speaking with the family members of a client who was a 19-year-old college student, I couldn't help but wonder if the mother was also an alcoholic. Sensing that I'd detected her drinking patterns, she voluntarily agreed to a 30-day period of abstinence and to attend AA meetings. Her drinking was more thoroughly discussed in family counseling while her son was in treatment. In this case, the mother's drinking had not progressed to where she couldn't participate in the intervention, even if it warranted further discussion.

Having both parents equally involved in an intervention is also particularly important. More often than not, it is the addict's mother who initiates contact with me. I always ask about the child's father and am encouraged when the parents are on the same page, regardless of their marital status.

The involvement of stepparents can be equally important depending on their relationship with the child. Your son or daughter may look up to their stepparent or may resent them for being married to their mother or father. In my preparation leading up to the intervention, I ask a lot of questions in the hope of getting a good understanding of the various relationships and how they will affect the person being intervened on. I'm also listening for things to use during the intervention which may compel the individual to accept treatment. You would be surprised how much information families forego during the initial assessment that pops up later during the intervention. Having this happen isn't necessarily a problem, though it can sometimes be beneficial to have this information earlier.

In cases where the mother says the father won't participate or isn't involved in their son or daughter's life, I usually suggest I speak with him myself unless the father has been absent for a long time. Some parents have been traumatized by their addicted son or daughter and have spent a lot of money paying for failed rehab attempts, attorney's fees, wrecked cars and education the addict failed or never completed. Even so, my intentions are to align the parents and encourage parents who have lost hope. I sincerely believe as long as someone is still alive, there is always hope they will recover and that relationships will be restored.

When selecting those who will participate in the intervention, you should choose participants who you know will be willing to follow directions and stay focused. Having an uncooperative participant who can't be trusted, won't stay focused or who wants to make the intervention about themselves or their resentments can result in an unsuccessful outcome. In addition to siblings, other examples like these might include resentful ex-loves or former friends.

Typically the point person or primary contact between the family and interventionist will decide who should and should not be there (though in some cases there is discussion). The point person is usually the individual who initiates contact with the interventionist, but that is not always the case. Sometimes the point person naturally emerges as the process gets underway. If you're leading the intervention yourself, you are both the point person and the interventionist.

As a third-party interventionist (someone who's not normally part of the family or a family friend), I have a blind spot: I only have access to information provided by the family members and participants.

Regardless of all the questions I ask leading up to an intervention, things may still arise that would have been useful for me to know ahead of the intervention. If you lead an intervention yourself, one pro is that you shouldn't have too many surprises because you have firsthand knowledge of your child's history.

Deciding which family members and friends to involve in the intervention is going to be a question of judgment. Before speaking with prospective participants, ask yourself: "Will this person betray my confidence if not asked to participate?" If you're not sure about someone, speak to them generally, saying things like, "We're concerned about our son's drinking and" See how the conversation unfolds and if you're comfortable. If you are, then great; if not, there's nothing to worry about because you never mentioned the intervention.

You may have to think further about involving core family members and friends who struggle with substance abuse themselves. If your son or daughter's father is an active alcoholic, for example, that could affect the intervention; at the same time, not having him there is also a considerable deficit. In this example, I suggest asking the father if he can remain sober for the intervention and how he will respond when your son says, "I'm not going to treatment—Dad drinks three times as much as me."

The Covid-19 pandemic has also impacted how interventions are carried out and who participates in them. Pre-pandemic, it was assumed older parents and grandparents would participate in person. Covid-

19 has changed that, as it's much riskier for older people and people who are immunocompromised to travel on planes, stay in hotels and participate in group activities. Additionally, there may be people who don't want to travel simply out of precaution. These participants will have to join the intervention through video conferencing, or e-mail their impact letters to be read on their behalf.

Confirming Insurance Benefits (In-Network vs. Out-of-Network) and Paying for Treatment

Selecting the best treatment program for your child is very important. If you've already determined where they're going to treatment or if you're paying for treatment out of pocket, you can avoid the constraints of working with insurance benefits. With that said, most people try to use their health insurance to pay for treatment and therefore only want to consider programs that are in-network with their insurance company.

Before making treatment decisions, contact your health insurance company to confirm your plan's benefits for in-network treatment programs. Once the insurance company confirms your policy is current, they will redirect your call to the behavioral health department or a third-party insurance provider. Some major carriers contract with other insurance companies specializing in behavioral health. Still, be sure to avoid any 1-800 numbers that refer to treatment facilities.

When you call the insurance company, don't let the agents dictate which facilities you should call. Instead, let them know you want to see the whole in-network list for the country if need be and go from there. This process can be time-consuming and frustrating, so make sure you're ready to be on the phone for at least an hour.

The number of treatment centers taking insurance has steadily increased over the last few years because doing so provides them with a steadier flow of new clients. This increase of in-network providers is a positive trend as it gives consumers more options.

Insurance companies have pre-negotiated rates with in-network treatment centers—ask them for a list of these treatment options before calling treatment centers directly. Some plans limit their members to treatment facilities within their state of residency. Your insurance may be used for out-of-network benefits, which will increase your treatment options but will likely increase your out-of-pocket expenses significantly.

There will always be out-of-pocket expenses, and your insurance benefits may change at any time— even preauthorization doesn't guarantee that your child will get a full 30 days of residential treatment. You also need to know how much treatment will cost after your son or daughter's benefits are exhausted, in case they require a longer length of stay.

The number of covered inpatient days can vary widely from company to company and plan to plan. When speaking with a prospective treatment facility, make sure they carefully break down all the costs for you.

The first thing insurance-driven treatment centers will want to do is run your insurance to check your benefits. It's like a car dealer wanting to run your credit before letting you test drive a car. If their program is not in-network with your insurance company, they will refer you to another facility unless you're able to pay for treatment out-of-pocket.

If you're paying for treatment out-of-pocket and aren't restricted by insurance, a world of options opens up for your son or daughter. Paying privately for treatment gives you the advantage of negotiating better rates and making decisions solely on the level of care required—Negotiating private pay treatment costs is something I do for families all the time.

Even though the treatment facility has run your benefits, make sure to check them yourself. I like to check my client's benefits personally, but if the insurance company won't speak with me because I'm not on the policy, I have the mother or father call.

Insurance companies are usually willing to provide enough information for me to determine my clients' out-of-pocket expenses. You do not want a situation where you have to come up with a large payment or remove your son or daughter from a treatment program because of unexpected or unplanned expenses.

Make sure you determine what your co-pay and out-of-pocket maximum after your annual deductible has been met will be up front.

If you find an out-of-network treatment center, they will likely offer to run your out-of-network benefits. Still, these costs are generally significantly higher

Even when you have all the information in-hand, your benefits can still change. The costs you'll receive are only estimates, and your son or daughter is still required to go through a pre-screen interview before admission.

Depending on the situation, I usually put my client's son or daughter on the phone with the admissions personnel after the intervention, or in the car en route to the facility. Just remember: *there's always a chance your son or daughter won't meet the insurance company's treatment requirements.*

The pre-screen interview consists of several basic questions that demonstrate the patient's need for treatment. Some of the questions include:

- How often does the patient consume substances
- When was the last time the patient consumed substances
- Prior history of treatment or being arrested
- Has the patient ever considered suicide

Once the admissions team has this information, they can get pre-authorization from the insurance company. After your son or daughter gets admitted, it's not unusual for there to be several more days of back-and-forth about benefits between the facility and your insurance company.

Because the insurance company may only authorize a limited number of residential care days, the treatment center often has to continuously go back to request more time. Big treatment providers with multiple facilities track insurance authorizations and may be able to tell you what to expect. For example, they may quote you averages—they often see an average 21 days of residential care from BlueCross BlueShield compared to 28 days from United Healthcare, for example.

If your child is covered under your health insurance and you work for a larger organization, you're more likely to have better benefits. If you're an individual business owner and purchase your insurance independently, your benefits may not be as generous. Some of the more restrictive plans have higher deductibles and out-of-pocket maximums to be met before the insurer will cover the cost of treatment. This being the case, it may be better to negotiate a cash price. For example, if it's going to cost $14,000 to use insurance benefits, that money may be better spent at a higher quality or better-fitting program.

Depending on how busy a treatment center is, they may be willing to sell you 30 days of residential care for $14,000 (though if they are at capacity, they are less likely to discount the cost of treatment). Putting aside the therapeutic component, treatment facilities are still businesses that require capital to keep operating.

If the lowest price the treatment center can accept is $20,000 and you can afford to meet this cost, ask them for additional treatment days. Thirty days is not a lot of time, and any additional days of treatment will benefit your child. Different facilities may also allow you to make several payments in lieu of a single large payment.

It's rare to have no out-of-pocket expenses even with good insurance, so make sure financial matters are handled in advance of your son or daughter arriving at treatment—this is not something you will want to deal with when they arrive at midnight after a five-hour cross country flight.

I find most treatment centers are as accommodating as possible. People who work in the addiction treatment field want to see your child recover, and they will usually do everything within their power to make that happen.

Selecting a Treatment Center

Selecting the appropriate level of care for your son or daughter is one of the most important parts of the pre-intervention process. Making the wrong decision can result in your son or daughter feeling unmotivated and may create additional resentments that will have to be resolved. I don't expect anyone to enter treatment with the same enthusiasm they would have checking into a five-star resort, but their first impression should still be comforting.

As a professional interventionist, families rely on

me to have personal experience with the treatment facilities I recommend. I visit between 15 to 25 rehabs every year that offer the services and programming I believe contribute to achieving lasting sobriety. My experience has helped me establish credibility and rapport with parents and their families during the intervention.

The treatment facility you choose may ultimately be a function of your family's health insurance benefits or your ability to pay, as previously discussed. Residential treatment costs approximately $1,000 per day, so most families understandably make every effort to use their in-network benefits. In those cases, you will have to select the best program available within the parameters of your plan and personal finances.

A good treatment facility will offer a variety of programs and support services in a clinical environment conducive to recovery. Some essential features to look for are a strong focus on family systems, a full-time clinical team, on-campus detox, abstinence and 12-step based programming, an excellent reputation and active alumni participation. Any program with loyal alumni says a lot about the quality of care provided.

Some long-term treatment programs (90 days and longer) don't have on-site detox because it's too expensive to operate without a high volume of admissions. These programs use third-party detoxes to stabilize patients before admitting them to treatment.

I tend to favor treatment programs with residential buildings, a dining hall, and treatment facilities on the same property—similar to a college campus. This type of setting feels more comfortable and provides additional structure for patients. Above all, *I never recommend treatment centers I wouldn't feel comfortable sending my own daughter to or attend myself.*

It's often difficult to evaluate facilities by their websites alone. I recommend calling each one you're considering and speaking with staff members to help you get a better sense of the center. Don't be afraid to contact the program's executive director or clinical director—they should be happy to answer your questions to help you decide if their program is appropriate for your child. If they are not responsive or you don't feel comfortable speaking with them, then it's not the right place.

There's a marked difference in the quality of care between a treatment facility with an enthusiastic staff and a program where the staff are burned out and demoralized. I have experienced both, and naturally gravitate towards programs with positive energy.

Sometimes when I research facilities, I may ask to speak with alumni of the program or to parents of alumni. Treatment centers always have families who are happy to speak with prospective clients. If you're considering a long-term program, I would definitely recommend doing this.

Your son or daughter should feel safe when they arrive at the facility you choose. It's expected for newcomers to have a heightened sense of fear and defensiveness upon arrival; an environment that helps deescalate these reactions is good.

It's a good idea to avoid treatment centers that oversell non-therapeutic amenities and luxuries, such as 800-thread count sheets and gourmet chefs. These can contribute to your son or daughter's sense of entitlement and inflate their ego. Recovery is a spiritual journey where people seek conscious contact with their higher power; luxury amenities are not part of the spiritual experience.

High-end treatment facilities can be effective for executives and other high-earning professionals because they create an environment that makes them comfortable, affording them greater flexibility to focus on their professional responsibilities. Generally speaking, executives are not the demographic we're focusing on in this guide.

Speaking personally, I arrived at the Betty Ford Center in 2004 with some very grandiose ideas and acted like I was checking into the Four Seasons or a five-star European cruise. Had the treatment facility given me the luxurious experience I was hoping for, it would have contributed to the progression of my disease by inflating my ego and further delaying my recovery.

Treatment centers spend a lot of money to acquire even a single patient. By some accounts, these costs can run approximately $5000 per person. As a results, treatment facilities do whatever they can to reach the greatest number of prospective families from every corner of the United States. This is why searching for rehabs in New York can return two pages of facilities in Florida and Arizona. It's also like looking at houses on real estate websites—the photography and content are designed to make everything look attractive.

Beware of programs that don't emphasize the therapeutic experience or have loose policies around technology. Some programs use experiential therapies as part of their therapeutic approach. This may include ropes courses and other outdoor activities that can have a positive effect when combined with other evidence-based therapies. Experiential therapies seem to be especially productive for young people.

A trusted resource that I regularly use is the National Association for Addiction Treatment Providers' (NAATP) Addiction Industry Directory. If the treatment center you are considering is not a member of NAATP, it's a good idea to remove them from your list as this organization requires its members maintain a certain quality of standards.

Two other accreditations to be aware of are The Joint Commission and the Commission on Accreditation of Rehabilitation Facilities (CARF). Like the NAATP, these organizations require their members to maintain set standards to display their seals.

People in treatment require structure and strictly-enforced boundaries to aid their recovery. Each facilities policies and protocols are purpose-driven and in place by design. Some of them include strict technology policies, scheduled times for calling home, proper attire, wake-up times and bedtimes, requirements that clients keep their rooms clean and beds made and rules against fraternization.

Your son or daughter will inevitably call home to tell you "how bad things are" and that "they would rather be in prison than in treatment." I want to assure you they are likely doing fine. If you have carefully researched treatment options and followed the guidelines provided here, there's no reason for you to doubt the treatment choice you've made. I encourage you to trust the process and remain hopeful for a successful outcome.

Length of Treatment

Length of treatment is an important consideration that often gets pushed aside because of financial limitations. Some families are hesitant to impose a treatment program beyond the generally accepted 28 days. Other families may feel getting their son or daughter into any program accomplishes their goals regardless of other considerations.

For many years, the standard of care was based on a 28-day model that has been popularized in television shows and movies. However, the current standard of care has shifted closer to 90 days to one year—and there are good reasons for that. Advancements in technology have allowed researchers to observe the addicted brain in real time to see exactly how it is affected by chemical dependency. This same technology shows us it takes at least one year for the brain to recover from addiction.

Is any length of treatment better than no treatment? Yes! If your insurance company will only authorize a shorter length of stay such as 14 to 30 days, you should of course take it. Though I am obviously a proponent of treatment (and longer is better), there are millions of people who have gotten sober without going to treatment. These are men and women who walked into the rooms of AA, sat down on hard metal folding chairs and drank disgusting black coffee as they detoxed and began to recover.

Regardless of where your son or daughter goes to treatment, whether it be the most expensive program in Malibu or the Salvation Army, people who stay sober go to Alcoholics Anonymous, Narcotics Anonymous or some other abstinence program.

People in early recovery (less than one year of abstinence) are highly susceptible to relapse, so the longer they remain in treatment or another structured environment, the better their chances of long-term sobriety.

Along the same lines, some treatment facilities have eliminated smoking and vaping from their campuses because of how nicotine irritates healing neurotransmitters and activates cravings. Every time a recovering addict smokes a cigarette or puffs on a vape, it's like scratching a nagging itch that can become increasingly more irritating.

How long your son or daughter remains in treatment will likely be determined by how much your insurance company is willing to pay and your ability to afford the expenses of additional care. While your insurance company may only authorize 30 days of residential care (and sometimes less), they may, for example, offer to pay for an additional month of outpatient treatment.

In the ideal situation, your child will remain in a residential setting for up to 90 days, followed by outpatient treatment and structured sober living for an one year or more. The idea is to keep them in a safe environment for as long as possible before returning them to the outside world where drugs and alcohol will be a greater temptation.

Though it's not uncommon for addicts to return to treatment multiple times before getting sober, long-term treatment is effective in avoiding the danger and emotional turmoil that ongoing relapses can have on the individual and their family. Families I speak with are often tempted to adopt a wait-and-see position in lieu of initiating an intervention, hoping the situation will improve on its own over the next few months. What they don't realize is the recovery timeline is more realistically comprised of many years.

Without taking specific and deliberate action to get your son or daughter into treatment, their disease will advance unabated. The number of true addicts who are able to stop using without professional help is extremely limited. There's no reason for you to believe your child is one of the lucky few, and by the time you are fully convinced they need more support than you can provide, it may be too late.

Some insurance policies are obviously better than others for behavioral health benefits. If you work for a big corporation your benefits may be generous;

however, if you have an individual policy, they will likely be more limited.

Mental Illness and Dual Diagnosis

Many people who struggle with addiction also struggle with mental illness. Most treatment facilities are equipped to address both addiction and mental illness simultaneously, also known as dual diagnosis treatment. If your son or daughter has a history of mental illness and traumatic episodes, remember to be vocal about that when vetting treatment centers.

After hearing your child's history, treatment facilities should be able to make a determination if their program is a good fit or not. In some cases, they can also recommend other programs. Be aware that many treatment centers will say they are licensed to treat mental illness or have a track for eating disorders or trauma, but what this really means varies from facility to facility. Be sure they have experience in the issues you're seeking help for before committing your son or daughter into care.

Geography Matters

The location of the treatment center you choose is important as well. Parents often want their children to stay close to home so they can visit and participate in their recovery. Generally speaking, this is a mistake. I advocate for sending children to treatment facilities far away from home because it reduces the risk of them leaving prematurely and against medical advice (also known as leaving AMA).

Putting distance between you and your child is also useful in preventing them from manipulating you. The same parents who initially want their children nearby quickly realize the benefits of having them at a distance. After years of sleepless nights, these parents can return to resting more easily knowing their children are in the care of competent professionals.

As an example, I once placed a 23-year-old from Ft. Lauderdale in a treatment facility about an hour drive outside of Dallas. The program was an appropriate fit for him—it was in network with his insurance company and was located in the middle of several cattle ranches far from civilization. One afternoon, I got a phone call from this young man's treatment team saying he was threatening to walk out.

This news didn't overly concern me because I'd planned for the occasion by putting him in the middle of a bunch of cow pastures to begin with. My response was to let him go—perhaps he needed a long walk to think things over. The kid stuffed his belongings in a hardshell suitcase with a missing wheel and proceeded to walk down the road. The treatment facility contacted the client's mother and she immediately started calling and texting me.

This went on for a little while and I started getting concerned. While I felt confident counseling the treatment team and the mother to not negotiate and let him walk, newly recovering people still do stupid things. About two hours into the episode, I got a call saying the young man returned and was willing to cooperate. Had we placed him in a treatment center in South Florida, he may have made it home or gotten in touch with his dealer—in which case we may never have gotten him back.

Pre-Intervention and Intervention Agendas

The pre-intervention and intervention agendas are in place to guide participants through the process of getting their child into treatment without being distracted by anything unimportant. When I'm working with a family, pre-intervention is an entire day of hard work, because often we're pausing to process any feelings or concerns anyone has. When making the agendas for pre-interventions, each one should contain specific information about the following:

- Addresses of meeting locations (hotels and otherwise)
- Dates and times (eg., "prior to the intervention, participants will meet at 8 am")
- Responsibilities for specific tasks (eg., "Tara will bring "addict" into the living room")
- Travel information (departure and arrival times for participants' flights);
- Time to practice reading impact letters (including role-play of potential reactions)

- Time to discuss participants' feelings
- Potential reasons "addict" will refuse treatment (and potential responses)
- How the group will handle outbursts or escape attempts
- Who will help the "addict" pack for treatment

I recommend asking participants to watch *Can Love Survive Addiction and Codependency* before the intervention as well—it is available for free on South Florida Intervention's official website.

The evening before the intervention, I take family members to a local Al-Anon meeting and encourage them to share about the upcoming intervention. Though anyone is welcome to attend, it's required for immediate family members—parents, siblings, children and spouses. If you have trouble finding an Al-Anon meeting, participants can attend an open AA meeting.

It's okay to take some creative license when drafting agendas. Consider adding in exercises like meditation or asking participants to share past experiences of doing presentations in front of coworkers or delivering bad news to people. Be sure to ask what tools they used to make the task easier for them.

If your family and the participants are religious. build in time for prayer in the agendas as well. I've had family members ask about prayer during interventions, and I encourage it—it can be comforting for the participants and the interventionist alike. Though you should do whatever is most familiar for your family members, prayer can be extremely powerful for some people.

For the non-religious, there are non-denominational prayers in the "Big Book" of Alcoholics Anonymous you can use during the pre-intervention and intervention. The Serenity Prayer is particularly relevant to any family struggling with addiction:

God, grant me the serenity
>   to accept the things I cannot change,
>   the courage to change the things I can,
>   and the wisdom to know the difference.

However you decide to prepare for the upcoming intervention, remind yourself that it's coming from a genuine place in your heart. You will not have a response for every defense mechanism your son or daughter throws at you. Some of their excuses may not even be rational explanations, but none of that matters or should shift you away from getting them into treatment.

Arranging Transportation to Treatment

Assuming your son or daughter is going to treatment out of state, you'll have to make transportation arrangements in advance of the intervention. Waiting to buy plane tickets until after the intervention is cost-prohibitive and may cause unnecessary delays, giving your child the opportunity to change their mind about going to treatment.

As an additional tip, consider buying airline tickets that allow some flexibility, even if they're more expensive. Interventions can go on longer than anticipated, and your son or daughter may have to detox locally before going to treatment. I recommend flying Southwest Airlines almost exclusively because of their liberal ticketing and cancellation policies. Buying the cheapest ticket on most airlines typically means having to buy new tickets at the last minute or paying exorbitant penalties for making changes.

Failing to deliver your son or daughter to treatment immediately after the intervention could mean having them at home for one or two additional days. It's going to be difficult for you to keep them from drinking and using drugs during that time. Knowing it's their last night to get high, there's a greater chance of them accidentally overdosing or getting picked up by the police during a bender.

Always select nonstop flights—stopping to change planes provides another opportunity for your son or daughter to get in trouble and adds unnecessary logistics to the journey. Some treatment facilities will have someone meet you as you're getting off the plane to make the last leg of the trip easier.

You also have to know who will be escorting your son or daughter to treatment before the intervention. It obviously has to be somebody you trust and somebody who's willing to take responsibility for getting them there safely. This person should be somebody who won't be easily manipulated or overwhelmed by the responsibility. A sister or brother or trusted cousin may be a good person to carry out this responsibility.

Because addicts can go from reasonable to irrational in a split-second once drugs or alcohol enter their system, it is important for the addict to be supervised from the start of the intervention until the time they're admitted into treatment. Obviously, this includes time spent at the airport and on the plane.

If you will be escorting your son or daughter to treatment, make sure you sit together on the plane and don't allow anyone to manipulate you into sitting separately. It may be necessary to alert the flight attendants not to serve your son or daughter during the flight as well.

As mentioned before, sometimes it may be better to allow your son or daughter to drink or continue using drugs on the plane so they don't have a seizure or begin withdrawals before getting into detox. Having this agreement in place means they may be less inclined to sneak off or ditch you in the airport to drink or use drugs. Even so, this isn't explicit advice to allow your son or daughter to drink and do drugs on the way to treatment. That's a decision that has to be made personally, though if you do make it, be sure to have a system and a plan in place.

In those cases, set limits such as one drink per hour of flight time, or allow them to use the minimum amount of drugs necessary to keep them settled. If they can't agree to these parameters or need to drink and use drugs to the point of intoxication, it may be better for them to detox locally before going to treatment. If for some reason it's necessary to keep them at home for an additional night before going to rehab, don't let them out of the house unattended. In the best case scenario, they're going to drink and get high. In the worst case scenario, their last hoorah might result in a fatal overdose.

If they are not in good enough condition to fly commercially, consider taking them to a detox facility two or three hours away from home to decrease the chances of them walking out when they start feeling better. For example, if you live on Long Island, take them to a detox center in New Jersey and make arrangements for them to fly out of the nearest airport or drive directly to treatment from there. Do not allow them to return home before going to treatment; small demands like making a quick stop at a friend's house to say goodbye may feel harmless and reasonable, but the reality is they may be getting drugs or manipulating the situation. It's important to remain a couple of steps ahead of them at all times.

Most professional interventionists offer transportation services or can recommend professional transport. Having an experienced escort will cost $1500 to $3000 or more, plus expenses depending on how much time is required. If you don't have any good options, paying for this service may be a good investment.

Writing an Impact Letter

An impact letter is a critical form of communication that intervention participants read during an intervention. The letters are written to convey how the addict's addiction has impacted them personally. As a parent, your impact letter will carry special importance, particularly if your son or daughter isn't married and doesn't have their own kids. If your child is an adult with their own family, letters from a spouse or children will likely be the most pivotal.

I often say my clients mostly consist of scared parents and pissed off spouses—parents are terrified they'll lose their child to drugs, whereas spouses are often angrier at their partner than afraid. The love between a parent and child is self-sacrificial and irreplaceable. The love between spouses, on the other hand, is intended to be mutually beneficial and tends to be more conditional.

Impact letters allow you to express your concern for your son or daughter in a compassionate and nonjudgmental way while at the same time letting them know how serious their circumstances are. While you may feel anger and frustration towards them (as many parents do), an intervention is not the appropriate place to punish, embarrass or shame them. The only goal for that day is to get them into treatment safely.

Once they're in treatment, you will have further opportunity to process how your son or daughter's behavior made you feel—and that while you still love them, it's understandable that you're also angry. Though these tough feelings can be processed during family week, during the intervention, saying things that will heighten the addict's sense of fear or make them more defensive is counterproductive.

Not all impact letters read during the intervention need to threaten consequences. The intervention can also include participants like family friends and clergymen. Some people will be there to bolster core family members and lend their own influence. In some ways, I think of these people as the "outer circle," and have them read their letters first. Though these letters can focus on the impacts of addiction, they can also recall memorable experiences from better times to lift the atmosphere in the room.

When putting together an intervention, I'm reluctant to have outer members threaten serious consequences over relatively frivolous issues. In some cases, these smaller gripes can derail more serious issues that core family members bring up, and can start the intervention off in a more confrontational way than is necessary.

Proceeding inward, the next circle of letters can be from aunts, uncles, cousins, close friends or even the addict's employers. Close aunts and uncles are often respected members of the family, and best friends and employers are also important relationships that carry a lot of weight in interventions—especially if the addict is at risk of losing their job. Similarly, hearing they're at risk of losing a close friend can be a real eye opener as well.

The inner-most circle consists of core family members like parents, spouses and children. The order of these letters is determined by who has the greatest level of influence or who is best positioned to implement consequences. This varies from family to family, regardless of age. I've attended interventions for married men who were unmoved by their wives' threats but were scared to death of their parents. In my own intervention, my parents were certainly very influential, but it was the threat of losing my wife and two-year-old that scared me the most.

Before sitting down to write the impact letter, think about what you want to say. Try jotting down some notes for a few days leading up to writing the letter. In general, aim to write a letter that you would still stand behind if were read to you five years later— at a time when the person of concern is recovering and thriving.

Below is a sample impact letter I share with my clients prior to the pre-intervention meeting:

Dear Michael,

It seems like only yesterday you graduated from high school and prepared for college with your whole life ahead of you and the world at your feet. Everybody looked up to you, especially me. When you graduated college with top honors, nobody was surprised at your success in academia. In fact, it's exactly what we expected from a superstar like you.

Right after college, you were offered a once in a lifetime opportunity to move to New York City and pursue your dream of becoming an architect at one of the city's most prestigious firms. Here again no one was surprised at your early success.

We always assumed you would make great things happen. As time went on, we started hearing less from you; at first, we chalked it up to long hours in the office and hard work, but then we started wondering if there was something else. You stopped returning telephones calls or coming home for the holidays. We wondered if you had become a big shot and wanted to leave the memories of small-town America behind.

The truth was ultimately revealed when your brother Jack went up to New York City to look in on you. He was surprised to learn about your drinking and daily use of prescription drugs. To be honest, we were angry when Jack reported all of this, but then our anger turned to hurt and many nights of lost sleep.

We wondered if one day the police would call informing us our eldest son had died of a drug overdose or in an accident. When you lost your job in New York and moved back home, we thought things would be different—until you were arrested for driving under the influence.

Bailing you out of jail that night almost destroyed me. You were no longer the superstar you were only a few years earlier. Working odd jobs for little money and not being able to keep a relationship is not the man you were meant to be.

We prayed you would stop drinking by yourself or that you would meet a nice girl and get married, but neither has happened in almost 10 years.

A couple of months ago, our fear of losing you became too much for us to bear and we started looking for ways to help you. We are here to ask you to accept help and go to treatment today. Michael—will you accept this special gift?

There are no strict rules for writing an impact letter as long as it is sincere, non-confrontational and intended to encourage recovery. To reiterate an earlier point below is an example of how a parent may describe a past occurrence which impacted them:

Ever since finding you unresponsive on the bathroom floor over the summer, I have found myself struggling with anxiety, because I can't stop thinking about what it would be like to lose you. Recalling the paramedics rushing into our house plays over and over in my mind.

The closing part of the impact letter must clearly specify a consequence if your son or daughter refuses to accept the family's request for them to go to treatment that day:

Michael, if you choose not to accept treatment today, I will have no other choice than to ask you to move out of our family's home. Having to ask you to leave will be very painful for me and will no doubt make you angry, but I would rather you be angry with me than see you dead or behind bars because you hurt an innocent person. I love you and hope you will go to treatment today.

Practice reading the impact letters at the pre-intervention meeting. Doing so will help you get comfortable delivering your personal message and will mitigate some of the fear you'll likely experience. The more you rehearse reading the impact letters at the pre-intervention, the easier it will be the following morning.

Keep rehearsing until everybody is comfortable, which may require more time for the immediate family members than some of the other participants. Above all, don't be afraid to discuss how you're feeling —sharing a feeling makes it less onerous. There's even a saying in Alcoholics Anonymous that addresses this: *a feeling shared is a feeling halved.*

Use a Timeline to Demonstrate The Problem

Prior to the pre-intervention, make a timeline of your son or daughter's life relative to their addiction. Include events that not only directly correlate with substances, like being arrested for driving under the influence, but also that demonstrate unmanageability, like being fired from jobs or failing classes they should have gotten high grades in.

You don't have to include every stumble they've experienced in life unless the event was of particular concern. For example, when I was 16 years old, I got thrown off a teen tour in Israel. I was years from discovering drugs and alcohol, but the event clearly demonstrated my inability to follow directions and avoid consequences, even after receiving a warning, which is addict behavior.

After graduating college, I went through several jobs in quick succession. Some of them were good opportunities, but I ran from each one at the first feeling of discomfort. Neither of these examples on their own suggest I would become addicted to drugs, but both were indicative of a pattern which demonstrated my need for help. I would quickly accept jobs which had no correlation to my skills or interests because I didn't know how to manage my anxiety about not working. Even so, I would then become resentful pretty quickly and quit.

Later, there were undeniable problems associated with my drug addiction starting in my late twenties. It started with stealing money to buy pills, inappropriate behavior, staying up all night getting high, lying about my drug use, being fired from jobs, having debilitating panic attacks, shopping for doctors, depression, low self-esteem, fear of impending doom, being kicked out of the house and struggling with a highly contentious and failing marriage. I was never in trouble with the police because my drug of choice was amphetamines, and when I drank, I mostly did so at night alone at home. In essence, I avoided the police merely through dumb luck.

I could continue ad infinitum, but you get the picture. Using myself as an example, the above timeline tells a revealing story of a person struggling to get along on life's terms. It also shows how I attempted to use drugs as a solution to my problems. Like many people who struggle with addiction, I was relieved when I discovered that taking a couple of pills temporarily took my troubles away.

In your own intervention, your child may offer

excuses for what caused each of these events as well, and perhaps some of them will be legitimate explanations. Even so, all the information put together will tell a clearer picture. The objective is to show them how they will benefit from treatment.

Choosing and Implementing Consequences

In the ideal situation, your child will agree to accept treatment based on the benefits of sobriety rather than the threat of consequences. Though this positive outcome happens more often than you may think, you can't count on it happening at your intervention.

I've led many successful interventions without having to speak of consequences—the individuals were simply ready to end the nightmare their addictions had become. I've also been in situations where people agreed to treatment just to avoid consequences and had no intention of remaining sober. There are times I want to see an individual experience consequences so they can internalize the seriousness of their situation. I think of these people as "doing time" rather than getting well.

The most common reason a person refuses to accept treatment is fear. They are afraid of what life will be like without drugs or alcohol. All the excuses they offer are a cover story for their fear. Your son or daughter sees drugs and alcohol as a solution and you see it as the problem. This a very common divide between addicts and those encouraging them to accept help.

Whatever reason your child gives for accepting treatment, my hope is they start to understand the benefits of sobriety through the process. Perhaps they will see themselves reflected in a fellow patient, or simply decide they want a better way of life.

Still, your child may need a compelling reason other than the promise of a better life to accept treatment. Sometimes they are too stubborn to admit drugs and alcohol are not working for them, or their ego won't allow them to concede defeat. In such cases, it's necessary to impose consequences.

Imposing a consequence is equally as punishing for the parent as it is for the child. If you tell your child they have to leave the family home, this may mean you'll have some sleepless nights ahead of you. Not knowing where my daughter is would cause me a great deal of anxiety.

What's important to remember is that threatening a consequence you're not prepared to carry out will damage your credibility. For example, if you are not willing or capable of removing your child from your home, do not threaten to throw them out.

I have worked with wives who said they would throw their husbands out if they didn't accept treatment, all while knowing from our conversations that they weren't being realistic. In other cases, another woman may genuinely have no hesitation throwing her husband out because she has emotional and financial wherewithal to follow through.

An alternative to permanently ending a relationship is issuing a consequence which stands until the individual agrees to accept treatment. Even so, be careful navigating consequences like these. A good manipulator may find wiggle room in these kinds of deals, but carried out carefully, this tactic can be very effective.

I once worked with a family where the wife had spent years tip-toeing around her alcoholic husband. She was hesitant to even speak with me when we started working together. Little by little, she started gaining courage. During one of several discussions, she told me she would never leave him. I responded by asking her if she pledged to never leave, how would anything ever change?

I knew she and her adult children were the most important participants in the intervention we were planning, and we had to come up with a consequence she could stand behind. Before the intervention, I asked her if she would agree to leave the family home and discontinue communication with her husband until he was admitted into treatment. With eager anticipation, she said, "I can do that!"

As that experience showed perfectly, failing to set and implement consequences will only reinforce the behaviors you're seeking to eradicate. Just remember: only threaten consequences you're comfortable enforcing if they refuse treatment, such as taking away their car or cutting them off financially.

Every person experiences pain at a different threshold. Because of this, one consequence may be immediately effective for one person but have no effect on another. In my own life, I acquiesced at the first mention of consequences while one of my best friends in recovery had to lose his marriage, career and home before surrendering.

Selecting Venues

Selecting an appropriate venue for the pre-intervention meeting and intervention shouldn't be too difficult, nor should you get too bogged down in these details. If participants are coming from out of town and staying at a local hotel, simply have the pre-intervention meeting there.

Regardless of where participants are coming from, the best venue may be your own home provided your child isn't living with you. Otherwise, ask one of the participants if they can host the pre-intervention meeting. In other circumstances, your church or synagogue may be able to accommodate you, or you can rent a suite at an inexpensive hotel. Perhaps you may even have access to a conference room you can use elsewhere—be creative, but use whatever works.

The intervention should be held early the following morning at your child's home, where they can easily be found. This eliminates the risk of having to lure them to a second location, which will make them suspicious or have them not show up. You want the plan to be as simple as possible and to avoid anything elaborate. The closer you stick to the truth, the better off you will be.

Anytime you have the opportunity to eliminate a moving part, take it out. The same thing is true for anything that may be considered unreliable. If there's a non-essential participant who is chronically late or untrustworthy, try to avoid involving them. If the participant is critical to the success of the intervention but unreliable, assign someone to keep them accountable.

Getting Help for Yourself and Other Family Members

Getting help for yourself and other family members is vitally important and goes back to making good treatment decisions. I put tremendous emphasis on choosing treatment facilities that have committed the time and resources to develop effective family programs, and I cannot stress enough how important this approach is to achieving lasting recovery.

If you're reading this, you should already be attending Al-Anon meetings. Al-Anon was created to help family members affected by addiction to recover from codependency using the 12 Steps. It's a free program and is readily available in most communities.

The availability of 12-Step meetings, including Al-Anon, has been significantly reduced as a result of the Covid-19 pandemic. This unprecedented reduction has made things difficult for families new to recovery, since meetings are almost exclusively being held online.

I personally started attending Al-Anon when a family member close to me began struggling with addiction and mental illness. The program helped me to allow this person to have their own journey without me trying to control them, fix them or blame myself for their behavior.

Despite the benefits Al-Anon provides, it's often harder to get parents to go to Al-Anon than it is to get their sons and daughters to Alcoholics Anonymous or Narcotics Anonymous. Lastly, family members who need additional support may consider Codependents Anonymous (CoDA) for codependency issues or Families Anonymous.

Whatever you decide, don't make the mistake of thinking of your child's addiction as siloed, existing in a way that has nothing to do with you. Addiction is a family disease and a systemic problem. It must be confronted that way.

Who Should Lead the Intervention?

Deciding who will lead the intervention is an important decision. Whoever accepts the position must embrace a great deal of responsibility and risk. If the intervention goes badly, you will probably blame this person and possibly lose the relationship. In order to successfully do their job, the person acting as interventionist will have to set themselves apart from the other participants and maintain authority throughout the intervention.

As a professional without pre-existing attachments to the family, I don't have to concern myself with preserving personal relationships—this gives me a greater ability to do my job. The person you ask to lead the intervention may have to overcome their normal role as a sympathetic family friend or fondly-regarded uncle to become an impartial leader. For example, your child is going to make several hard-fought attempts to take the spotlight off themselves and turn it on you for whatever past transgressions you may have committed. It's up to the leader to prevent this from happening and refocus the intervention back where it belongs.

An inexperienced leader may see this distraction as relevant and allow it to continue to the point of failure. A trained professional will immediately see it for what it is and quickly squash it. In a properly executed intervention, there are very specific goals which have to be accomplished throughout the day and distractions only take away from that.

As your child's parent, you may have assumed you will lead the intervention; however, you can't be the interventionist and the parent at the same time. It's too difficult for you to separate yourself from being an invested parent and become an effective, objective leader. I include myself when I say parents are no good when it comes to their own children. For those reasons, it might be easy for me to see your relationship with your children clearly—even though I remain baffled by my own daughter.

That's not to say a parent can't have a meaningful conversation with their son or daughter that results in them going to treatment, but that's not what we're talking about here. We're talking about hosting an intervention for a person who is treatment resistant, meaning they are either committed to not accepting treatment or don't believe they need it.

In any case, a clergyman or rabbi can often work and is a better choice than one of the parents. The leader can also be a trusted aunt or uncle. Take your time to make a considered decision—once you appoint someone to the leadership position, you cannot change your mind during the intervention and takeover yourself.

Meeting Before the Intervention

The day of the intervention is always nerve-wracking for the parents and participants. On intervention days, I take a few minutes to mentally prepare myself for the upcoming event before meeting up with the participants. I contemplate staying present in the moment and responding to challenges with patience and grace rather than ego.

During the pre-intervention, I repeatedly tell participants to expect to be met with resistance. Once your child realizes they're in danger of losing their drug of choice, their addicted brain will send out a distress signal telling them to head to their battle stations. Their hostile reaction will be driven by fear —they can't imagine how they will survive without their drug, which they believe is the solution to their problems.

On a personal note, I felt the same way as many of the young people I help when I was addicted. When I took my first pill, I felt the weight of the world melt off my shoulders. I had been looking for something to make me feel better about myself my whole life. Initially, the idea of having my solution taken from me was terrifying.

Approach the intervention with empathy and remember that no matter how nervous you are, the person being intervened on is many times more afraid. Don't forget that you've been planning the intervention for days or weeks and understand the situation. Your son or daughter just woke up 15 minutes ago and are coming into the situation on their back foot. In other words, you know what's about to transpire and have had time to contemplate the intervention; your child is the one walking into a surprise.

Resist the urge to respond to personal attacks or to your child saying they refuse to accept treatment. Maintain the integrity of the intervention regardless much they try to disrupt the process. Ask them to sit quietly and consider what everyone has to say. Ensure them they are safe and that nothing bad is going to happen to them.

One day, your son or daughter may look back at their intervention as a an "act of God" moment, but they are highly unlikely to have the ability to recognize the significance of the moment until they are sober and have gained clarity. In my own experience, there were many miraculous moments in the early days of my recovery at the Betty Ford Center, but I didn't have the ability to recognize them for what they were until much later.

If your child is being woken up from a cold sleep, allow them a few minutes to go to the bathroom. If you know they drink coffee right after getting up, have it ready for them—same with cigarettes or food if they need to eat right away. If they have to pop a pill to be functional (as I did first thing in the morning), allow them to do so. Demonstrate goodwill, but stay focused and keep your structure and boundaries firmly in place.

On the day of the intervention, participants should be prepared to meet first thing in the morning at a location convenient to where your child resides. As the interventionist, I arrive ahead of everybody else; the person leading the intervention should do the same. It's also important to have the participants' mobile numbers readily available. When planning interventions, staying organized is an essential element of success.

When Your Child Enters the Room

Participants should arrive at your child's house together, enter as a single group and immediately carry out their assignments. Remember that some participants should set up the living room (or other meeting area in the house) while some of the others collect your child from their bedroom.

It's hard to know how your child will react when they walk into the intervention. You need to be prepared for them to be surprised and afraid, or for them to try to run away. Though I've seen very few people run, there still needs to be a plan if this happens.

Their most likely reaction is to be speechless as they process what's taking place around them. After the addict is calm and acclimated, I like to seat the intervention party in a horseshoe shape with a space for the individual between the two people they will be most comfortable with. Typically, this is their nuclear family, their mother and father or wife and children.

Because I start interventions early in the morning, the individual usually has to be woken up and escorted into the room. Here again, I designate the least threatening two people to wake up the individual. If they have a close sibling or favorite cousin participating in the intervention, recruit them to get them from their bedroom.

Your son or daughter will be caught off guard if the person waking them up has come home from college or is someone who wouldn't ordinarily be there. Even so, this can be positive because it alerts the individual that something out of the ordinary is happening and it tends to get them moving a little faster.

As the leader of the intervention, I remain standing and greet the individual as they enter the room. I introduce myself as an addiction interventionist and then gesture for them to sit in their designated spot. If they are confused or ask what is happening, I reassure them they are in a safe place and everybody is here today because they deeply care for them. I then ask them to please sit down because their family has something they want to say.

Drug Testing and Narcan

I carry 16 panel drug tests in my knapsack along with Naloxone, better known as Narcan, which is a nasal inhalant that can temporarily reverse an opioid overdose in case of an emergency. The drug test screens for a wide variety of substances. *If your son or daughter is an opioid or heroin addict, make sure you always keep Narcan within arm's reach at all times as a precaution.*

If your son or daughter is adamant about not being an addict, you can pull out the drug test, put it in front of them and say to them, "If you're not an addict, you won't mind taking a test." This is a risky move because if the test comes back negative, you will have created an additional hurdle for yourself.

Remember that a negative drug test doesn't negate your child's need for treatment. Just because they are not drinking or using at that moment doesn't mean they're not an addict. After all, using drugs and alcohol is only a symptom, and a lot of people go to treatment having already detoxed.

If you're confident your child is using drugs or drinking, having them complete a test can remove any remaining deniability—but it can also be a risky move. In the event you choose to test them, have someone go into the bathroom to make sure the urinalysis is properly collected.

What if They Run?

Prior to the intervention, I designate two people to chase the individual if they run. The "chasers" are usually two friends or other non-threatening people who the individual is likely to listen to. The chasers tend to be siblings, cousins or friends. I want the parents to remain where they are in hopes of quickly resolving the situation.

If the individual threatens to walk out, I might ask in a nonthreatening voice, "Where are you going? Are you going to walk out on your family?" If they walk out or hide in their room, I suggest letting them sit for

10 or 15 minutes and give them a chance to re-emerge on their own.

If the individual has a history of self-harm or suicide attempts, it's important to take steps to intervene even more quickly. In these situations, inform your child that if they threaten to harm themselves, the police will have to be called. Once again, if your child has a history of self-harm or suicide attempts, I advise against staging an intervention without the assistance of a trained professional.

Reading Impact Letters

Decide in advance in what order the impact letters will be read. Begin with someone important, but not the people who will implement the strongest conse-quences. The first couple of readers may not have consequences to implement because they are family friends or caring coworkers (which is okay).

If the individual is younger and living at home or unmarried and living separately from their parents, end with the parents. If the individual is married, end with the spouse and children (if they are old enough to participate). If the children are too young to participate but are able to express how they've been affected by their parent's addiction, they can write a letter that someone else can read at the intervention. The children's letters can simply express their love for their parent and their desire for them to get better—anything that reminds the addicted parent their drinking or using is affecting their child is valuable. The intention is to have the circle tighten as the intervention proceeds. The people with the most leverage should make the closing statements.

After Reading Impact Letters

After the impact letters are read, sit quietly for a few minutes. Give your child an opportunity to speak first. If they don't give a response, I usually say in a comforting voice: "I have gotten to know your family over the last couple of weeks and they love you very much." After that, I give them another opportunity to respond. Usually, this means asking how they're feeling about everything that has been said. During this follow up, keep things light and use non-threatening communication. Avoid escalating conflict if at all possible.

At this stage, I want to start moving the individual forward and may say: "The treatment center you are going to is located in Colorado. It's a fantastic place. I have been there a couple of times and people really love it. We are on a 12 pm flight to Denver—do you want your mom and dad to help you get ready?"

If the child responds with, "I want my mom to help me pack," I take that as confirmation of acceptance and say: "Do you want to give your mom and dad a hug and tell them you love them?" Always end on something positive.

If your child is married, I ask if they want their wife or husband to help them get ready. As long as they are moving forward at this point, keep the momentum going. The sooner you get them in the car with the person escorting them, the better.

If They Hesitate or Refuse to Go

It's understandable for your child to hesitate or be confused or afraid after hearing the impact letters read. After allowing some space for them to process what they've heard, keep explaining to them that they're in a loving and safe place with people who want them to get help.

In some cases, telling the child that they should listen again to a certain section of a letter to hear the love or caring can be a helpful strategy as well. If the child is still resisting or insisting that they don't need help at this stage, it can be helpful to switch into a "hot seat" exercise.

In a hot seat exercise, select someone important to the individual (such as their child or sibling) and place that person in the leader's chair. Explain to the addict that the person in the chair is suffering from acute addiction and is experiencing many concerning consequences as a result. After that, ask your child: Knowing that addiction is a potentially fatal disease, what is the appropriate decision to take for the person in the leader's chair?

Tell your child that they're in charge of the person in the leader's chair. Explain all the negative things that person is experiencing—whether its arrests, health problems, damaged relationships, financial trouble or whatever else it may be. Make sure the situation you're describing mirrors the situation your child is in.

Be direct in asking your child how to deal with this situation, one that is clearly a problem. Should this person simply try harder? Should they cut back? Should they deny help and try to make a go of it on their own?

In many cases, your child will see the difference and understand the correct solution: that person should get on a plane and go to treatment right away before the problem gets worse. When presenting these options, make sure to appeal to your child's sense of motivation.

To an addict, drug and alcohol use are not a problem; they are a *solution* to a problem. It's only to the loved ones and family members that the drug and alcohol use themselves are the problem. Viewing it from this perspective, consider the fear and anxiety an addict must face to give up a behavior that they view as helping them get through life.

Instead of presenting treatment as something the addict has to stop doing because it's bad, paint a larger picture of what kind of life treatment could help them to have. In reality, there is a way to lead a happy and fulfilling life without drugs and alcohol, even if the addict can't see that at the moment. If they could really see the truth, the difference between continuing to use drugs and alcohol and getting sober would be like the choice between a new car and a sack of coal.

Without escalating or getting aggressive, be sure to

explain the entire picture to them, cycling through relevant parts of the impact letters as necessary to make the points you need to make.

If your child responds by saying they are not going to treatment, do not be dissuaded; it only means they don't have sufficient information to make a decision yet.

Here is your opportunity to explore what is holding them back from accepting treatment. They may provide a logistical block, such as work or another obligation. These objections can be worked through. If they deny being an addict or alcoholic, review the timeline with them again.

In terms of self-directed interventions, this is where a lack of prior experience can become a handicap. Despite whatever excuse your son or daughter offers for not accepting treatment, as professional interventionist, I can usually share an experience, personal or otherwise, which reflects how they may be feeling.

My goal is to continuously offer inspiration and evidence of a better life. In fact, there's a powerful quote from Martin Luther King Jr. that I often think about while conducting interventions. In the interview, someone was asking if he thought he was teaching "Christian love" as part of his doctrine and what the relevance of that was. His reply was, "Yes, that's my basic approach. I believe love is the most durable element in the world."

Even for non-religious and non-Christian families, King's comment that love is the most durable element is certainly true—and it's that durable love that can help families successfully intervene for their children to help them overcome addiction.

Even if you lack direct experience as a recovering person yourself, find another way to identify with the person being intervened on. When my dad intervened on me over the phone, I automatically responded by saying I couldn't go to treatment because I was too busy (which was an exaggeration of my circumstances at the time). Despite my father's lack of experience, he recounted the story of going to the cardiologist and being diagnosed as immediately needing open heart surgery. The doctor told him if someone couldn't pick him up and take him directly to the hospital, the doctor would have to call an ambulance himself.

Unlike myself, my father was the CEO of a manufacturing company, had several real estate investments which required his ongoing attention and had a type-A personality. When he got his diagnosis, he had no opportunity to make arrangements for his absence, or let people know he was going to be away from work on medical leave for the next eight weeks. He had to undergo surgery within the next 24 hours, and his only option was to surrender and accept his own powerlessness. I look back at that moment as highly significant in my recovery, because unbeknownst to him, my father was teaching me about the first step:

"We admitted we were powerless over alcohol and that our lives had become unmanageable."

There may come a point during the intervention where it seems you have lost all forward momentum. Your child is sitting on the couch with their arms crossed, refusing to accept treatment. At this stage, it's important to refrain from begging them to accept treatment.

Begging them to accept treatment is not within the spirit of the intervention and it concedes authority. It's true we want them to go to treatment and we'll accept any form of acceptance they can muster; however, being in treatment is hard work, and it's not an all-expense paid vacation. Anytime a parent says to their child, "It's like an all-expense-paid vacation," I always add that treatment is hard work because I don't want anyone going in with the wrong expectations.

You do not want to give them permission to go to treatment just to mark off days on a calendar. They are not doing time—they are being treated for a life-threatening disease and they should know what is expected of them. I advise participants to avoid saying things like, "It's only 30 days and you'll be home before too long." The intervention is an opportunity for your child to start holding themselves accountable, and it may be the first opportunity they've ever had to really do so.

Successfully completing an intervention is often about allowing enough time for the individual to process and accept the circumstances around them. It is okay to continue reassuring the individual while maintaining structure and boundaries.

Regardless of their attitude at the intervention, the hope is always that their desire for sobriety will catch fire once they are in treatment. By interacting with other patients and seeing a reflection of themselves and their experiences in others, your child may ultimately decide a life of sobriety has more benefits than drinking or using, and that the benefits of sobriety outweigh the costs of active addiction.

The Turning Point

There may come a time during the intervention where you have read the impact letters, addressed their objections and sympathized with their fear. If at that stage they still won't commit to treatment, it's time to change course and tone. On the handful of occasions where an intervention reaches this point, it follows a lengthy discussion.

In such situations, I say to the individual:

"I want nothing more than to take you to treatment today so you can start living the life you were meant to have, but you have made the decision not to accept treatment and therefore must be willing to accept the consequences which were stated earlier in your family's letters."

This is the most difficult part of the intervention for any parent. At this point, you must implement the consequences laid out in the impact letters. If your consequence was for them to be removed from the family home, bring in the suitcase and offer to help them start packing. *Regardless of their reaction, you must not concede.*

If your child is married and their spouse's consequence is to remove them from the family home, you must be prepared to support the spouse like they're your own child, regardless of how you feel about them or however much you want to blame them for your child's addiction.

If you become sidetracked by irrelevant distractions or revert to blaming your son or daughter's spouse, the intervention will end badly. The same is true if you fail to implement the consequences you threatened in the impact letter.

If your child protests by saying they don't believe you'll throw them out, tell them:

> "Over the last couple of weeks, I've read a lot about addiction and now understand it's a life-threatening disease. Over 72,000 Americans die every year from untreated addictions. I love you more than anything, but I'd rather have you homeless than have to plan your funeral. I am at peace with my decision."

If your child's spouse has to ask them to leave the home, help them say something like this:

> "I have been living with your active addiction for years and will admit that I unwittingly contributed to your illness. I was angry when I should have

been offering you professional help, but you're being offered that right now and you're choosing not to accept it. Over the last couple of weeks, I have been attending Al-Anon meetings, which is a support group for family members of alcoholics and addicts, and I'm much more clear about what has to happen in order for our family to recover from addiction. I know there's no way you'll recover if I keep enabling you, and therefore I am asking you to leave the home now."

By beginning to implement consequences, your child will hopefully take you seriously and reverse their decision to refuse treatment. When they finally acquiesce, remind them why they're going and that treatment is hard work. Do not turn the situation into a standoff.

It may be the hardest thing you'll ever have to do throwing your son or daughter out of the house, but unless you want to see them spend the rest of their life in active addiction or die of a fatal overdose, remained committed to the intervention plan.

Common Excuses for Refusing Treatment

You are going to encounter many excuses during the intervention and some of them may be valid, so practice responding to them beforehand. If your child has a job, make sure you speak with their employer. If they're in school, make sure you have collaborated with their dean or guidance counselor.

Depending on your child's age and professional circumstances, exercise caution approaching their employer. If their employer is somebody you have a direct relationship with or is the person who initiated the conversation about there being problems at work, then generally it's okay to involve them.

If you have doubts about contacting your child's employer, consider it this way: would you hesitate to contact them if your child was in a serious accident and needed medical attention? Of course you wouldn't hesitate. With that being the case, the same thing applies here—addiction is potentially fatal if not treated.

There is a stigma attached to addiction and mental illness that does not apply to other diseases. Taking ownership of being an alcoholic or addict is humbling and potentially humiliating, but unlike other diseases, there is a guaranteed life-saving treatment.

I have had experiences where the employer approached the family about problems at work relating to drugs and alcohol but then refused to participate in the intervention. Some employers may see their getting involved as a liability issue.

In general, here are some common excuses I typically encounter during an intervention for refusing treatment; all of them can be successfully managed with some initial planning:

. . .

"I will go to treatment tomorrow." There's no such thing as "tomorrow" at an intervention. Unless your child is on the plane or en route to treatment as planned, the consequences described in the impact letters go into immediate effect.

"I have to work or attend school." As stated earlier, account for these logistical hurdles in advance of the intervention. Assure your child their school will collaborate with the treatment center so they don't fall behind. Treatment facilities that specialize in school-age clients in high school and college typically have an educational coordinator on staff that will communicate with their teachers.

When it comes to taking off work, the Americans with Disabilities Act (ADA) ensures that people with disabilities have the same rights and opportunities as everyone else. This includes people with addiction to alcohol and people in recovery from opioid and substance use disorders.

Additional protection is afforded by the Family and Medical Leave Act (FMLA), which says eligible people are entitled to take unpaid, job-protected leave for specified family and medical reasons with continuation of group health insurance coverage under the same terms and conditions as if the employee had not taken leave.

Practically speaking, once your child agrees to treatment, they will have to contact their employer and inform them of their decision. If your child has a job with many responsibilities, you may have to contact their employer before setting the intervention. If the intervention is the result of a near fatal overdose or accident, focus on getting them into treatment and deal with their career later.

"I just can't leave my children." This is a valid objection, and you better be prepared with a satisfactory response—especially if your grandchildren are young and it's their mother going to treatment. I can't tell you what the answer should be because every family's circumstances are different. Childcare can be less concerning if it's the father going to treatment, provided the mother is capable of taking care of the children, but this also depends on age, marital status and the family's economic situation.

"I can't go to treatment because of coronavirus." Coronavirus is new to the list of objections, but it could be replaced with whatever the newest world crisis is. Nonetheless, it's no reason to postpone or cancel an intervention. In fact, coronavirus may be the perfect time for your son or daughter to go to treatment because there's no school and most people are working from home. It also saves them from having to explain a long absence to their coworkers or classmates.

. . .

"Who will take care of my cat or dog?" Someone will have to agree in advance to take your child's pet. Make sure this is worked out before the intervention.

"Who will run my business if I go to treatment?" This is an understandable concern for someone who owns a small business, and the answer very much depends on individual circumstances. Is there someone capable of running the business in the addict's absence? Can the business operate by itself with little involvement from the owner? These can sometimes be satisfactory solutions. In other cases, some treatment facilities are geared for business owners and professionals and allow the client a couple of hours each day for them to focus on their business.

If your son or daughter is a professional, such as an attorney or commercial real estate broker, having a couple of hours a day to focus on their business may be just fine. If their business is strictly hands-on (as it is for electricians or plumbers), they may have to make some very serious decisions about temporarily closing their business or setting up a forwarding telephone number to an honest competitor who can cover for them. Before going on vacation, doctors who have their own practices often ask other practitioners to cover them.

. . .

"I will go after my pending charges are dropped or reduced" *or* ***"I'm on probation and can't leave the county."*** As you would imagine, pending charges and probation are common issues in interventions. Always consult your son or daughter's attorney before doing anything, because taking them out of the state or county could violate their probation agreement. With this said, my experience has been that probation officers and judges are cooperative when it comes to allowing probationers to attend treatment.

If you contact your child's probation officer before setting up the intervention, they will most likely tell you there's a process which includes requesting permission from the judge to leave their jurisdiction. I have also seen people take off for treatment and not contact their parole officer until they've already been admitted into treatment, and that often works out too.

Though I can't tell you what to do, if my son were out every night shooting heroin and risking his life, I would be concerned first and foremost with saving his life and less worried about getting him in hot water with his parole officer.

"You promised never to send me back to treatment." Promising to never send your son or daughter back to treatment is unrealistic because they may relapse and require additional treatment. You wouldn't promise someone recovering from cancer to never send them back for chemotherapy.

Making this promise essentially grants them immunity to commit future violations. As an interventionist, I have no problem dismissing this objection. When they pull this card at the intervention, tell them it's a promise you should have never made and you're sorry for making it, but their circumstances are such that additional treatment is required—end of story.

You have nothing to feel guilty about. You're acting in their best interest and if that causes resentment, they can work it out in treatment with their treatment team. I tell families all the time that if their child is still resentful, they're not ready to leave treatment. If your child is more concerned about you going back on your word or getting "ambushed" at the intervention than they are about you trying to save their life, they need more time in treatment.

"Let me drink or use one more night and I will go tomorrow." Allowing them to go out one more time is possibly the most fatal mistake a parent can make. Think about what that last night out is going to look like—a no-holds-barred drug fest that could result in a fatal overdose, getting into trouble with the police and hurting themselves or somebody else.

If for some reason your child can't be delivered to treatment immediately following the intervention, make arrangements for somebody to get them away from home that day. I prefer for them to fly to where the treatment facility is and stay overnight at a hotel with supervision. Get them into a detox center or into another safe place where they can be monitored. Do not leave them anywhere unsupervised with money in their pocket.

The bottom line: don't trust them and don't test them. We already know what happens when an active addict is left to make their own decisions. Be overly cautious and don't leave anything to chance.

"I can stop anytime I want to." Ask the individual to give the participants three examples of when stopping on his own produced more than one year of sobriety or clean time.

"You have betrayed me by having an intervention." Ask the family to provide examples of when the individual has betrayed and or lied to them.

"I want to go on my own terms." Remind the individual they have had years to resolve their alcoholism on their own terms and have never produced a meaningful result.

"I haven't had a drink in two weeks" or *"I've cut down a lot."* Tell the individual this is a good step towards starting their recovery, but treatment for acute alcoholism and or drug addiction requires professional help to achieve long-term success.

. . .

*"**My drinking isn't hurting anybody**."* Ask the family to provide the individual with examples of how their drinking has damaged the family.

To an inexperienced interventionist, these excuses sound like valid excuses—but they are not. You will still need to be prepared to respond to them intelligently. If the circumstances were different and your child were being given an opportunity to do something they would enjoy (such as planning a last-minute trip to Europe), all the logistics would be easily worked out. Keep that in mind when they offer resistance.

Intervention Follow-Up

Once the two-day intervention is complete and your child has begun packing, collect the impact letters and ask the person escorting them to treatment to get the letters to the admissions person doing the intake interview. The letters are for your child to refer back to with their counselor or by themselves while in treatment. Reviewing the letters will help them work through any denial they may still be experiencing.

The letters also serve as a written reminder of the consequences your son or daughter could face if they fail to complete treatment as agreed. You can also scan the letters and email them once your son or daughter's counselor contacts you in the next couple of days.

On the first night of having your child in treatment, you can relax knowing they're in the care of trusted professionals. Still, on the second or third night, you can expect a call from the treatment facility saying that your child is threatening to walk out—and if they're at least 18 years old, there's nothing you can do to stop them. If you receive a call like this, tell them leaving is simply not an option and remind them of the consequences you set during the intervention. If they continue pushing you or not speaking to you in an acceptable manner, hang up the phone. Having your child in a remotely located treatment facility is a good idea in case conflicts like these arise.

As the interventionist who delivers clients to treatment, I typically receive these calls instead of the parents or families. Having a barrier between your child and yourself is useful for avoiding manipulation and unnecessary drama. Even so, be prepared to reiterate the reasons why they're in treatment and remind them of the consequences if they fail to successfully complete their program.

To avoid situations like these, ask a member of their treatment team to inform your child that if they walk away from treatment, the consequences in the impact letters will immediately go into effect. Hopefully, your child will have limited access to money and will therefore be forced to quickly reconsider their options. This is another important to make: before sending them to treatment, make sure their credit cards are turned off. Don't leave them with the ability to call an Uber or buy a plane ticket.

In treatment and while newly sober, patients are often fearful and compulsive. Their automatic response to discomfort may be to run or change their surroundings. It's the same set of feelings that cause them to drink when they don't feel good. Just remember: they are not yet well enough to know how to sit with their feelings and allow them to pass. Part of the process is to stay the course. Getting past the first week in treatment is a question of holding your boundaries and keeping the structure put in place at the intervention.

Dealing With Post-Intervention Resentment

At some point during treatment, you will be asked to attend the treatment facility's family program. This is when you will have an opportunity to speak more freely about how your child's addiction has affected you and other family members.

This is also an opportunity for your child to turn the spotlight back on you, and they may use this occasion to tell you how your parenting or personal defects contributed to their addiction. This face-to-face interaction is monitored by trained counselors who will refocus the conversation as needed, so it's not as perilous as you might imagine. It's likely that the treatment team will use the occasion to suggest additional treatment for your child, which is a suggestion you should take. They should also be leaning on you to attend Al-Anon meetings and focus on your own part of the recovery process.

The family portion of treatment tends to happen after your child has been in treatment for a while and is preparing to come home. If your son or daughter is still resentful at this point, *they're not ready to come home*. If their focus is on how they were "ambushed" or "lied to" at the intervention rather than on their life-threatening disease, *they have not begun recovering*.

If they feel this way, your child will likely do anything to prevent themselves from having to remain in treatment or move to a sober house. They will claim the intervention was an unnecessary and hurtful ambush which could have been avoided had you only taken the time to speak with them about their addiction.

These statements may catch you off guard, but try to avoid falling for this manipulation. Remind yourself how many times you've tried speaking with them about stopping their drinking or drug use. Ask them how many times they lied to you, stole money or caused you to lose sleep because they weren't home at four in the morning and weren't answering the phone or responding to texts.

Once you look at their post-intervention resentment in these terms, it will become clear how thin their argument is. Your child is in treatment because they suffer from a life-threatening disease. The better you understand the true nature of addiction, the less susceptible you will be to manipulation and guilt.

Post-intervention resentment is a dangerous trap, and I spend a lot of time with families preparing to manage these kinds of manipulations. Post-intervention resentment exploits the cracks in the foundation that causes the dam to come crashing down. As an example, I worked with a family in New York for several months preparing to intervene on their father, a formerly high-achieving individual turned full-time alcoholic. Under the influence of alcohol, this normally pleasant man morphed into a bully. He had previously been through a few well-respected treatment facilities and had trained his family to think each program was bad, hence why he had failed.

I had discussed the necessity of having a minimum year-long treatment term with the family at great length, particularly with the adult children and wife. Up to the intervention, the family had done a fantastic job preparing and plenty of positive changes were happening, especially in the wife's behavior. The intervention went very well and remains one I am most proud of. I took the gentleman to one of the best and most well-respected programs in the country, where he did quite well.

During the family program towards the end of treatment, he used the occasion to blast his family for ambushing him and claimed if they had only spoken to him sooner, he would have stopped drinking. The father did a masterful job taking the spotlight off his alcoholism and turning it on the family. That morning on Monday, I received a call from his adult children who felt incredibly remorseful, saying they had made a mistake putting their father in treatment.

"Let me see if I understand this correctly," I told the adult children. "Your father feels hurt that he was unfairly subjected to intervention and therefore believes his alcoholism should be allowed to carry on unabated and he should not be forced to go to sober living. It's like he got you on a technicality—the inter-vention was flawed so he should be allowed to go home and resume drinking with all charges dropped." I said this with utmost care and respect, but I couldn't completely hide my sarcasm. The adult children quickly understood my point, were empowered by our discussion and stood their ground.

At the same time, the father's counselor arrived back at work early in the morning, read the notes from the family weekend and arrived at the same conclusion as me. She got up from her desk, went to the resident halls and pulled the father out of bed. In a fairly strong manner, she explained how selfish and manipulative his behavior had been. The father broke down in tears and felt remorse for having held his family hostage over the weekend.

A couple of weeks later, the father was discharged from treatment and agreed to move directly in to sober living in New York. A couple of days after that, I got a group text from the wife saying she brought the father home the previous night because they were afraid he would be exposed to the newly evolving Covid-19. I responded to the group text saying I wish they had spoken to me first. Within 24 hours, the father was drinking like the intervention and treatment had never happened.

When Treatment Ends

Before your child leaves treatment, make sure you have an opportunity to clarify your expectations. Tell them relapse is not an option under any circumstances, and if they don't feel ready to return home, they should stay in treatment longer. Though what happens will largely be a dependent on your finances, it's better for them to stay in treatment long-term than come home prematurely and relapse.

Alternatively, they can go directly from treatment to a structured living environment such as a sober living home where abstinence and regular attendance at 12-step meetings are mandatory. Sober living is also less expensive than residential treatment.

If your child plans to return home immediately after treatment, make sure they know the consequences discussed during the intervention are still on the table if they start drinking or using drugs again and formalize them in an agreement. Inform them of this policy in advance of them returning home so they have time to consider what's best for them. Included in this agreement should be the right to drug test them on a regular basis. Testing on a regular basis will avoid them feeling like you are accusing them of relapsing. It's preferable to pay for a professional drug testing service so you're relieved of having to administer the test. If that's not possible, you can also purchase home tests in bulk online.

If you will administer drug tests at home, institute a random system for deciding when your child will get tested. For instance, tests could be administered every time an even number is rolled on a standard pair of dice.

Before they come home, have an agreement in place that dictates they attend 12-step meetings every day in person or online as circumstance dictate, with no exceptions. They should also be working with a sponsor who has at least two years of uninterrupted sobriety. Similarly, their sponsor must have a sponsor, and depending on the age of your child, you can ask them to introduce you to their sponsor and grand sponsor. If your child is using the tools they learned in treatment and are earnestly working towards their first year of sobriety, they shouldn't object. With that said, be sure to respect your child's privacy and be careful to avoid appearing critical if they're being compliant.

After completing treatment, it's up to your son or daughter to find local meetings which will be part of their weekly schedule. Aside from not drinking and using drugs, attending meetings is the most important thing newly sober people can do. Every part of a recovery program is important; however, the number one thing people say after returning to Alcoholics Anonymous following a relapse is they stopped going to meetings.

Thanks to technology, it's easy to find 12-step meetings, including Alcoholics Anonymous, Narcotics Anonymous and Al-Anon. Resources are readily available to everyone through a simple Google search. Any time I'm visiting a new location and want to find a meeting, I Google something like "AA meetings Dallas, Texas" and the result immediately includes a website and contact information.

This is very simple, so there should be no excuses for not attending meetings even when traveling. If your child fails to find a meeting, it's because they didn't want to find one. Sometimes getting the gumption to go to a meeting is difficult, just like it's hard to motivate yourself to go to the gym. Even so, once you're there, you're always happy you came.

Sober Living

Before your child completes treatment, consider having them go to sober living which is a less structured version of treatment that allows them to start integrating back into normal life without the pitfalls of too much freedom.

Sober living homes are located in most metropolitan areas and create a safe environment for newly recovering people. They are discreetly located in residential neighborhoods and are gender-specific. They may consist of four or five bedrooms which are typically shared by two residents each, with one of the bedrooms reserved for a house manager—generally someone recovering from addiction but who has been sober for several years. These environments have rules which often include getting up at a certain time, leaving the house at a certain time to work or look for work, a curfew, daily house meetings and regular attendance of an outside 12-step program. Drinking and using drugs are strictly prohibited, and anyone caught doing so will be made to leave the house that night no questions asked.

The First Year of Recovery

While you may have the expectation that your child will do everything they can to stay sober in their first year, you will also have to meet certain expectations and remain accountable. For parents, this means doing things like attending Al-Anon meetings regularly and perhaps attending family counseling. The better you understand yourself and your behaviors, the higher the likelihood of positive results in the long term.

Through therapy, you may discover things you were never aware of before. You may realize that it's your inability to implement consequences or maintain boundaries with your child that's leading to dysfunctional behaviors. In other cases, maybe it's your own unresolved childhood trauma playing out in your relationship with child. In both cases, these are negative patterns that can unintentionally contribute to their drug addiction.

Depending on the age and marital status of your child, some of the responsibilities that typically fall on the parents may be picked up by their spouse. If your adult children have kids of their own, they may need to be involved in recovery as well, depending on how old they are.

My daughter had just turned two when I left for treatment, but later, we took her to the Hazelden Betty Ford Foundation Children's Program when she was 10 years old to learn about addiction. The motivation for doing this was partly educational, but also because she had been subjected to traumatic experiences as a baby. My wife and I had some ugly fights during that time, and I had often been absent, depressed or acting out.

Conclusion

The thing about recovery is that we never graduate; it's a lifelong process. While my first year sober was difficult, it was also highly rewarding. My personal growth was exponential. At eight years sober, I struggled with new challenges and between years 13 and 14. I felt lost and couldn't see a clear path forward. If I had graduated from being a recovering alcoholic and addict at the end of my first year or fourth year, I probably would have returned to drinking.

The last lecture I attended in treatment before discharge was given by an alumna who had been through the same program a few years before me. She cautioned the group against having false confidence. "In here it's easy," She said. "You're not going to drink in here but hold onto your ass, because it's a wild ride out there." She was absolutely right.

Since then, I have stood at the same lectern and cautioned patients just as I was cautioned years before. I warned them that if they weren't careful, some of them might not make it past the airport bar on the way home before turning back for a drink. On the other hand, I said, some of them might feel strong for a couple of days or even a couple weeks before craving a drink. As a result, it was necessary not to allow any break between leaving treatment and attending meetings at home.

Above all, the point is that recovery is ongoing, and the threat of relapse is always present—and often unpredictable. Some recovering addicts relapse and find their way back to sobriety quickly, while others pick up a drink and spend years before making it back. Finally, there are some who pick up the bottle again and never make it back. The only way to beat it is to stay vigilant and to trust in the process.

Whatever the result, I applaud your courage for fighting your child's addiction issues head-on. The best advice I can give is to remain committed to the boundaries and consequences you put in place, no matter how badly you may want to relent. To that end, I'm providing a copy of the sobriety agreement and relapse prevention I use for my own clients at the end of this book. Use it as a guideline, though please feel free to customize it to meet your needs. If you stay organized and give yourself sufficient time to construct a smart intervention, I'm optimistic that you will have a successful outcome.

Additional Resources

Codependents Anonymous: www.coda.org

SMART Recovery: www.smartrecovery.org

Refuge Recovery: www.refugerecovery.org

Exhibit 1: Sobriety Agreement

Get help now!
(561) 961-4033

Sobriety Agreement and Relapse Prevention Plan

This sobriety agreement and relapse prevention plan are intended to assist you in achieving long-term sobriety and provide a simple guideline for building a healthy lifestyle by stating your responsibilities and those of your support system.

This agreement dated, _____ , by and between _____ (hereinafter referred to as "Recovering Person") and _____ (hereinafter referred to as

"Family"), shall commence upon execution hereof and remain enforce for twelve (12) months from the date above, however this term shall automatically restart in the event the Recovering Person's sobriety date changes.

In example only, if the Recovering Person's sobriety date is June 5th, and he or she relapses on September 1st, the term of this agreement automatically extends through August 31st of the following year; in other words, this agreement shall remain enforced until the Recovering Person achieves twelve months of uninterrupted sobriety.

Successful completion of this agreement includes:

1. Attend no less than one (1) 12-step meeting per day for the first three hundred and sixty five (365) days of sobriety, including holidays and special occasions for the term of this agreement; these meetings must be tracked and signed by the meeting chair or treasurer;

2. Identify and begin working with a sponsor who shall have no less than two (2) years of continuous sobriety; have a sponsor they regularly work with; have completed the 12 Steps; and be willing to work with you to complete the 12 Steps;

3. Commit to a regularly scheduled homegroup meeting and obtain a service position at that meeting;

4. Take medications as prescribed by a licensed physician, psychiatrist, or psychopharmacologist and attend all doctor's appointments as scheduled, including aftercare, IOP and PHP;

5. Comply with random drug testing either at

home or through a professional drug testing company as agreed;

6. Maintain paid employment at an appropriate business or organization, providing it does not sell or serve alcohol, including wine and beer, any type of tobacco or vape products, or any establishment where the culture may be conducive to drug and or alcohol use; a designated member of your support system may veto any employment they feel is not within the spirit of your recovery;

Designatee: _____

7. Abide by all reasonable rules set forth by the homeowner(s) of your place of residence, including parents, spouses or significant others, such as curfews, stealing of money or personal property, behaviors, invited guests, physical violence or threatening verbal exchanges; in the event the homeowner(s) or others feel threatened they may choose to call to the police;

8. Members of your support system have your permission to contact these people if they have reason to believe the Recovering Person has broken their sobriety, including, but not limited to your sponsor, pre-approved members of your sober network, interventionist, and or the treating physician;

Contact 1:
Telephone: 123-456-7890
Contact 2:
Telephone: 123-456-7890
Contact 3:
Telephone: 123-456-7890
Contact 4:

Telephone: 123-456-7890

9. If approached by a member of your family or sobriety network who inquires about the status of your sobriety, meetings, and/or sober activities, you agree to listen and respond in a productive and non-threatening manner.

In accordance with this agreement the Family agrees to provide the following support:

1. Encourage good sobriety with positive recognition, love, and support;
2. Remove alcohol and other addictive substances from the home, including Schedule II prescription medications and tobacco products if necessary;
3. Contribute to a calm and safe environment by practicing good communications skills instead of yelling or disempowering the Recovering Person by pointing fingers, use "I" statements (for example, "*When you vape at home, I feel unwelcome in my own home*")
4. When reasonably possible, provide transportation or the necessary money for transportation for the Recovering Person to attend 12 Step meetings, work, and doctor's appointments;
5. Regularly attend Al-Anon meetings family therapy sessions and focus on their own recovery.

SIGNATURES

RECOVERING PERSON
Name:
Date:
Signature 1:

DESIGNATED FAMILY MEMBER
Name:
Date:
Signature 2:

Exhibit 2: Meditations

Over the years I have come to regard many of the meditations regularly repeated in the rooms of Alcoholics Anonymous as making me feel as if I am home. Two of those meditations, "The Promises" and "A Vision for You" in particular, have a special meaning for me.

The Promises

The Promises describe the spiritual malady people in active addiction suffer from when first getting sober, these feelings for example are, regretting the past, feelings of uselessness, self pity, selfishness, self-seeking, fear of other people and economic insecurity, and confusion, but it also offers hope if we do the work to stay sober. Those promises include, freedom, happiness, peace, serenity, an improved attitude and a reliance on God, all which can be achieved by any person who wants it.

If we are painstaking about this phase of our development, we will be amazed before we are halfway through. We are going to know a new freedom and a new happiness. We will not regret the past nor wish to shut the door on it. We will comprehend the word serenity and we will know peace. No matter how far down the scale we have gone, we will see how our experience can benefit others. That feeling of uselessness and self pity will disappear. We will lose interest in selfish things and gain interest in our fellows.

Self-seeking will slip away. Our whole attitude and outlook upon life will change. Fear of people and of economic insecurity will leave us. We will intuitively know how to handle situations which used to baffle us. We will suddenly realize that God is doing for us what we could not do for ourselves.

Are these extravagant promises? We think not. They are being fulfilled among us—sometimes quickly, sometimes slowly. They will always materialize if we work for them.

A Vision For You

The second meditation, A Vision for You, can be found on the last page of the basic text of Alcoholics Anonymous, written in 1930's, and prescribers the solution for lifelong abstinence from drugs and alcohol. It says the person who suffers from this chronic disease must give up self-reliance, trust God and pass it on to the next person who suffers. Most importantly it encourages the reader to never give up regardless of how hopeless their situation may appear, which brings me to my final thought and something I truly believe; as long as your son or daughter is still alive there is always hope for their recovery.

Abandon yourself to God as you understand God. Admit your faults to Him and to your fellows. Clear away the wreckage of your past. Give freely of what you find and join us. We shall be with you in the Fellowship of the spirit, and you will surely meet some of us as you trudge the Road of Happy Destiny. **May God bless you and keep you—until then**.

About the Author

Marc Kantor got sober in 2004 at the Betty Ford Center and is the founder of South Florida Intervention, which helps families struggling with the effects of addiction to find lasting solutions.

For more information about staging an intervention, visit southfloridaintervention.com. Reach Marc Kantor at 202-390-2273.